Eco Ethics

Robert Stevens

This is an IndieMosh book
brought to you by MoshPit Publishing
an imprint of Mosher's Business Support Pty Ltd
PO BOX 147
Hazelbrook NSW 2779
www.indiemosh.com.au

Title: Eco Ethics
Author: Stevens, Robert
ISBNS: 978-1-925353-36-5 (paperback)
           978-1-925353-37-2 (ebook – epub)
           978-1-925353-38-9 (ebook – mobi)

Eco Ethics

What can Biology tell us about how we should live?

Robert Stevens

Contents

Preface

What can Biology tell us about how we should live? Biology has much to tell us. First, Biology – the study of life and living processes – teaches us about the nature of all living things. Biology tells us that all living things – from the tiniest bacteria, to vast ecosystems such as the Great Barrier Reef – are characterized by having purposes of their own. They are good for something: that is they are purposeful and valuable. Thus they should be treated with great respect, indeed reverence. We should watch our step.

Second, Biology is a source of rich and wonderful stories about humanity and its place in nature. It has a great deal to tell us about our own human nature and our identity - who we are. This has implications for our well-being and how we should live. Biology tells us that humans are highly social animals. Individual humans are part of a greater social whole – a social body. In common with insect societies, human societies are characterized by complex divisions of labour, supported by extensive cooperation and communication. We, in common with social insects such as ants, are not separate from each other but are interrelated. In common with ants, nothing we do makes sense except in the context of the society in which we live. In common with the social insects, our well-being is not an individual thing but depends on the flourishing of the social body of which we are a part, and the flourishing of other individuals in that social body.

Humans are part of more than just a social whole. We are part of a greater whole encompassing all Earthly living systems. We are part of the Milky Way Galaxy, the solar system, and the Earth. Earthly carbon, hydrogen, oxygen, and nitrogen cycles run right through us connecting us with all living beings. Not only are we connected to all Earthly living organisms spatially, but also temporally. Every individual human is a component of a number of lineages: sapiens; Homo; Primates; Mammals; Vertebrates; Animals; Eukaryotes and organisms, stretching back 4 billion years to a unicellular common ancestor.

Our flourishing is enhanced by recognizing this. Like all living systems, the purpose of an individual human is to live, live well and live better. Humans flourish to the extent that they have a sense of belonging or connection. We flourish to the extent that we see ourselves as whole and belonging to a bigger whole. Mere intellectual acknowledgement of our belonging is not sufficient for flourishing. That sense of belonging must permeate our lives, including our actions. Thus our flourishing depends on treating all living systems with reverence – on doing no harm. An ethical life is necessary to the good life. We should do no harm and we should also do good. But we should never do harm that good may come. We may be activists, but we must not use harmful means to achieve our good ends. For the sake of our own flourishing as well as all Earthly living systems we should walk more lightly on the Earth.

My reasons for writing this book are varied. I have long had a deep fascination for living things since childhood. A large, rather run down, musty-smelling old stone pavilion housing an eclectic botanical museum at the beautiful botanical gardens in Adelaide held a particular fascination for me as a child. Our family backyard was home to some lovely old almond trees and fruit trees and a variety of pets including Blue Tongue and Stumpy Tail Lizards, budgerigars, finches, bantams, rabbits and guinea pigs. I planted my own Zinnias as a child and watched enthralled as they developed. I have had a long fascination with ants and bees. The colony of bees in the glass bee-hive at the Museum of South Australia was a marvel to me, and has endured in my memory. This love of living things was reinforced and given a theoretical framework by some excellent teaching of Biology in high school. I was an enthusiastic member of the Natural History Club. At university I put Biology to one side and I developed a love of Philosophy that has stayed with me ever since. Within Philosophy my favourite subject was Ethics – looking at how we should live. My Doctorate, completed around 30 years ago, was in Ethics or more specifically political philosophy. A shortage of tenured positions in Philosophy Departments in Australia and internationally made me re-think an academic career, so I became a public servant and have been one ever since. I am now a Manager of Schooling Research in the New South Wales Department of Education.

I started working on *Eco-Ethics* about 15 years ago. Several developments prompted me to write it. My spiritual path in life changed from Christian to Buddhist. Buddhism, with its emphasis on inter-being and reverence for all life, re-kindled my interest in the living planet. Along with Feminism, Buddhism also challenged my whole approach to doing Philosophy. The tradition of Philosophy in which I was versed was analytical philosophy, that was steeped in assumptions about dichotomies between mind/body, culture/nature, reason/emotion, fact/value, life/death and, I was shocked to find, male/female. Where I used to see dichotomies, I now began to see continuities. A related development was that my politics changed complexion from pink to green.

Another development that inspired *Eco-Ethics* was a growing sense that the human-centredness of the field of Ethics is rather bizarre. If an alien life form just had Earthly books on Ethics to go by, the alien might be forgiven for thinking there was only one species on Earth – human beings. In most books on Ethics (the works of Peter Singer and some Environmental Ethicists being an honourable exception) of all the diverse species of Earth, only humans are worthy of mention. Most contemporary Ethicists regard values such as beauty, goodness and rightness to be human inventions. These things supposedly did not exist before humans. Furthermore, humans are supposed to be the only living things on the entire planet with any value of their own. The view that there was no value around before humans invented it has long seemed to me in tension with a Darwinian view of life as a single 4 billion year old tree, and humanity as just one small off-shoot of that tree.

So I decided to write a book on Ethics as if there were living species on Earth besides humans. At the same time I indulged my old love for Biology.

My final reason for writing this book is to articulate and to share the wonder of what Biology tells us about life on Earth, and how we are part of that great wonder. Biology, perhaps more than any other science, weaves a rich and wonderful story about who we are – our identity - and where we belong in nature – our deep connection to all living systems, past and present. It is a story that can give us great reverence for life. If we embrace this story, and let it permeate our lives, it can greatly enrich us.

I wish to thank the following people for their comments and contributions to earlier drafts of this book: Chris Barker, Geoff Barnes; John Bennett; Paul Brock; Raewyn Connell; Shanthi Clements, Andrew Dowling; Frank Elvey; Ruth Elvin; Judith Flanagan; Suzanne Frazer; Deb Frew; Olga Gostin; Harshi Gunawardena; John Hadley; Doug Mason; Debra Panizzon; Andrew Rolfe; Margaret Simons; Greg Snook; Tamara Stojanovic; Louise Trevillion; Rachel Watkins; Graham Wood; Carolyn Wells and Cheryl Williams. I also wish to thank Ally Mosher for her excellent design work.

Introduction

What does Biology – the study of life and living processes – tell us about how we should live?

One common answer to this question is simply "Nothing". Biology involves the discovery of *facts* about life and living processes. It does not involve making *value* judgments. Biology is the study of the living fabric of the world – the science of living matter. Values – such as good, bad, right, wrong, beauty, ugliness - are not part of the fabric of the world.

This negative answer to the question is backed up by various prevailing views about the source of value. Historically there have been two kinds of views. The first is that the source of value is transcendent – it comes from beyond nature, for example, from God. The Divine Command theory is one such theory applied to Ethics. According to that theory what is right is that which is commanded or loved by God (or the gods).

In Plato's dialogue *Euthyphro* Socrates argues that this view faces a dilemma. Either what is loved by the gods is right because it is loved or loved because it is right. If it is right because it is loved, right and wrong becomes arbitrary (if the gods loved murder then murder would be right). If the gods love what is right because it is right, then what is right is independent of the gods – that is, it is loved for features it has in itself apart from its being loved. [1]

Plato himself appears to have believed that values are transcendent. Values such as good, justice and beauty do not exist in their pure form in the physical world but exist in a transcendent realm. These values clearly interact with the physical world and may be palely reflected in the physical objects we see around us. It is only through deep contemplation that good, justice and beauty can be seen in their pure form. As Socrates rhetorically asks in *The Symposium* "What may we suppose to be the felicity of the man who sees absolute beauty in its essence, pure and unalloyed, who, instead of a beauty tainted by human flesh and colour and a mass of perishable rubbish, is able to apprehend divine beauty where it exists apart and alone?" [2]

Although these views about the source of value differ, Plato's theory and the Divine Command Theory both conceive of the source of value as transcendent. It comes from beyond nature. On either view, Biology is the study of the physical realm and values do not exist in the physical realm – they belong to a transcendent realm.

A very different view about the source of values is that they arise not from a transcendent realm but from humanity. Value is rooted in human nature, the human condition or human desires. According to one common view about the source of value, values arise from the valuing activity of human beings. Not only do we observe objects and events in the world but we are constantly evaluating them. Some we like and some we do not.

Think of beauty. Beauty, arguably, is in the eye of the beholder rather than intrinsic to an object. One person may find a work of music beautiful another may perceive it as just noise. Who is to say that one person is right and the other wrong? How could we decide? It comes down to a matter of taste. But if beauty is subjective why not other values such as good and bad, right and wrong? This is not to say that there are not objectively agreed standards of good, right and beauty. But these standards are artificial – they are invented. There would be no good or bad, no right or wrong, no beauty if humans (or their intellectual equivalent) did not exist. Beauty in a diamond for example appears to depend on a perceiver in a way that physical properties – such as the arrangements of atoms in a diamond – do not.

On this view, Biology is an objective science. But there are no objective values. All values are subjective. Goodness and rightness – like beauty – is in the eye of the beholder. To put it slightly differently, it is commonly asserted that Biology views organisms, including human beings, as physico-chemical mechanisms. There does seem to be, so far as science is concerned, nothing but atoms in varyingly complex arrangements. Values do not seem to fit into this materialistic world-view.

So we have three diverse and prevalent views about the nature and source of value and each of them, despite their differences, would insist on a strong fact/value distinction. Biology can tell us lots of facts about life and living processes but it can tell us nothing (directly at least) about values and how we should live.

Previous attempts to draw ethical conclusions from Biology have been less than convincing in hindsight – and often downright despicable. Sometimes biological notions have been employed to lend support to the need for one group to exercise power over another, and for the entitlement of one group to certain social privileges denied to another group, based on the supposed superiority of the former over the latter. In other cases, supposed scientific facts have been employed to demonstrate the inevitability of, or give credibility to, a utopia.

For example, Charles Darwin's theory of evolution has been used in the late 19th Century to justify capitalism (albeit not a rampant capitalism) in the writings of Benjamin Kidd, socialism in the writings of Karl Pearson, and anarchism in the writings of Peter Kropotkin. [3] In the hands of Kidd and Pearson, it was employed to justify western imperialism and the inevitability of the European domination and (inadvertent and regrettable) extermination of the "inferior" races. [4] Darwin's theory was the inspiration for the eugenics movement advocated by his cousin Francis Galton. [5]

All of this would seem to weigh heavily against the viability and desirability of a project to examine what Biology can tell us about how we should live.

Having said this, for a number of reasons the idea that values – in particular, good and bad - are not part of the fabric of the world, seems to me dubious. Similarly, the idea that Biology involves the discovery of facts about life and living processes but does not involve discovery of values – what is good and bad – also seems doubtful. My reason for doubting these popular doctrines is that as James Barnham points out "It is entirely natural to describe biological processes as functions that operate according to a means-ends logic. Functional ends or goals constitute norms with respect to which the means chosen may be judged good or bad, right or wrong, successful or unsuccessful." [6] If so, the supposed dichotomy between fact and value is somewhat fuzzy.

Chapter One: Purpose

The living world is full of wonders. Beneath the pippala tree, the hermit Gautama smiled and looked up at a pippala leaf silhouetted against the blue sky. "Looking deeply at the leaf, he saw the presence of the sun and stars – without the sun, without light and warmth, the leaf could not exist. This was like this because that was like that. He also saw in the leaf the presence of clouds – without clouds there could be no rain and without rain the leaf could not be. He saw the earth, time, space and mind – all were present in the leaf. In fact at that very moment, the entire universe existed in that leaf. The reality of the leaf was a wondrous miracle." [7] So Vietnamese Buddhist monk Thich Nhat Hanh describes a realisation of Gautama Siddhartha under the Bodhi tree.

Modern Biology confirms the Buddha's insights. The reality of the cosmos in a leaf makes sense in the context of the way the leaf is organised to collect and transform light from the sun, water from the cloud and carbon dioxide from the air into living matter. Modern Biology reveals that organisation and purpose permeate the living world.

The living world is thick with purpose. All living systems [8] from the tiniest bacterium to an ecosystem are permeated by purpose. All living systems are *organised* to achieve certain purposes or ends such as survival and reproduction. What is meant by the term "organise"?

The *Macquarie Dictionary* defines "organise" as "To form as or into a whole consisting of interdependent and coordinated parts, especially for harmonious or united action." To say that living systems are organised to achieve certain ends is in part to say that they operate according to a means-ends logic. Additionally, it is to say that the parts of living systems work together - *cooperate* - to achieve the ends of the whole.

The basic process of life is the process of cooperation and harmony, not competition and disharmony as is sometimes suggested. As one Biologist puts it "Disharmony can never be more than froth on the deep current of life. A system of relations so extensive and intricate remains intact solely in virtue of the harmony that pervades it; to saturate it with strife is to ensure its dissolution. In structures, in functions, in emotions, harmony is the pulsating heart of life; discord, the armour it puts on to confront the world." [9]

More specifically, to say that a living system is organised is to say that:

1. the parts work together to achieve the purposes of the whole
2. the parts have specialised functions contributing the achievement of the purposes of the whole
3. cooperation results in synergies – outcomes and payoffs of cooperation for the parts. For example, working together the parts of a living system

achieve what could never be achieved acting individually
4. the parts are dependent on each other for achieving their own purposes
5. the parts share resources equally with other parts of the system
6. the parts communicate with each other in carrying out their specialised functions

Some writers use the term 'design' where I have used 'organisation'. A problem with the term 'design' is that to talk of design seems to imply an intelligent designer – by analogy with human artifacts. Many of the writers who use the term 'design' in relation to living systems are card carrying atheists who do not accept that living systems have an intelligent designer. To avoid this implication, some writers say that living things give the *appearance* of having been designed for a purpose. [10] Others flank 'design' with quotation marks. The difficulty (for me) with this approach is that it is not always clear whether talk of apparent design implies that the design is merely apparent, purpose or both. As mentioned already I do want to argue that all living systems have a purpose. But I do not wish to assume that living systems have an intelligent designer. (They may have but they may not.) I like the term "organisation" because of its connection to other vocabulary used to describe living systems, such as "organism", "organic" and "organ". It helps us to avoid thinking of living systems as being machine-like and thinking of them as more life-like. As I will argue later the analogy between living systems and mechanical systems is quite limited.

Some examples may help to illuminate the meaning of "organisation for a purpose". I will illustrate the concept by reference to organisation in: multicellular organisms such as trees; a plant cell; Superorganisms such as leaf cutter ant societies and ecosystems such as the Amazon Jungle or the Great Barrier Reef.

Multicellular Organisms

Multicellular organisms such as trees are organised for a purpose. A tree is a living whole consisting of many different parts such as leaves, roots, a trunk, branches, inner and outer bark, flowers, fruits and seeds all in relationship with each other. Leaves are solar collectors. Combining carbon dioxide from the air and water from the soil, they use light from the sun to photosynthesise sugars – food for the tree. These sugars are used as an energy source for the tree's activities, and they form the bulk of the materials from which the tree is made. These sugars are transported to where they are needed in the rest of the tree through the inner bark. The roots absorb water and minerals from the soil. The mineralised water is pulled through the wood of the tree to the leaves – the principal users of the water. The minerals are used with the sugars to build essential components of the tree including the flowers, fruits and seeds needed to start the next generation. [11]

At a more fundamental level, a tree is a multicellular organism – a colony of cells. A mature pear tree contains 15 trillion cells. [12] A mature giant sequoia tree consists of 2 million trillion cells. [13] These cells work together – cooperate - to achieve the purposes of the whole of which they are a part, such as the survival and reproduction of the tree, and at the same time, their own survival and reproduction. Trees are thus collective survival and reproduction enterprises. [14]

British Physiologist Denis Noble writes "A characteristic of multicellular life is cellular harmony – in a healthy organism they must cooperate in harmonious ways in the interests of the whole, despite the fact that they also have their own 'selfish' interests…" [15] This cellular harmony commonly involves a *division of labour*. A standard example of a division of labour used by the 18th century economist Adam Smith is organisation of labour at a pin factory. Smith observed that ten workers allocated ten different tasks were able to produce nearly 50,000 pins per day. He imagined that if they were to work alone rather than together, each performing the ten tasks, that they would not be able to produce one pin per person. Peter Corning claims that this standard example of a division of labour does not reflect the importance of an organised labour process – a *combination of labour* – in which specialised skills, tools and production operations are combined into an organised system. [16]

A tree consists of specialised cells, such as leaf cells, root cells, and phloem cells (cells in the inner bark of the tree stacked one on the other to form a tube through which sap flows to all parts of the tree) specialised sex cells and so on. The differences between leaf, root, phloem and sex cells are not attributable to these cells having different genes (a unit of heredity composed of deoxyribonucleic acid – DNA for short.) Each cell in a multicellular organism has essentially identical genes. Each cell originates from a single fertilised egg, through a process of cell division called *mitosis*, organised to transmit identical copies of genetic material to each daughter cell. Cell differentiation depends on different genes being active (switched on or off) in different types of cell. This depends on influences external to the cell. Cells in a growing multicellular organism reproduce, and for each cell like begets like. Root cells beget root cells; leaf cells beget leaf cells and so on. Each cell has a dual inheritance system. One depends on copying genetic material and transmitting this to the next generation. The other involves copying and transmitting a state of gene activation. In a multicellular organism such as a tree the activity of a particular gene in a cell can be influenced by factors originating outside the cell, in other cells. Proteins produced in genes of one cell can influence the state of activation of genes in another cell. [17]

From the point of view of an individual cell, being part of a collective survival enterprise makes sense. Each cell carries out tasks that benefit the whole. Further, each cell is released from having to do all of the tasks necessary for its survival that prevent it from achieving mastery in any one of them. One group of cells specialise in photosynthesis, another in reproduction, another in distributing food to all the cells in the tree as required. In other words, the combinations of labour (or specializations) result in synergies – such as benefits or payoffs for the cells that could never be achieved working alone. [18] Working together, combining their labour, teams of cells accomplish more in terms of individual flourishing than could ever be accomplished by operating separately or independently.

The parts of the wholes are dependent on each other. Cooperation produces synergies, but it also creates interdependence and an individual stake in those synergies. The more valuable the synergies produced by cooperation are, the more likely we are to become dependent upon them. The parts become dependent on each other, and their fate becomes tied to the overall performance of the whole. Each part is also completely dependent on the other part; no part could exist without the services of the others, and only together can they survive and reproduce successfully. [19] They 'must cooperate' since they are all "In the same boat." [20]

As Noble notes "Complicated systems generally tend to regulate themselves by feedback effects, that is, by a process in which higher level (systems) parameters influence lower level components". [21] A tree as a whole regulates the activities of its parts. A tree has a highly organised internal control system for allocating resources to growth, maintenance and reproduction. This regulation is not centralised with any particular component. There are no privileged components telling the rest what to do. [22] There is rather a form of democracy, with every element at all levels having a chance to be part of a regulatory network. For example, a tree balances shoot and root growth. The shoots provide food for the roots and the roots provide water and minerals for the shoots, so there needs to be a balance between roots and shoots. An excess of roots become a burden on the food producing capacity of the leaves; an excess of shoots may overstretch water and nutrient availability. Trees have the ability to fine tune the ratio of shoots to roots. For example, if some of the leaf canopy is broken off, some of the roots die. If roots have difficulty in growing because of shallow soil, the leaf canopy remains small. [23]

Colonies of cells – that is, multicellular organisms – share water and nutrients equally between all component cells. Each cell carries out specialised tasks that benefit the whole – but the deal appears to be that whatever benefits the whole should also benefit each cell. Within a tree, each cell's needs are taken care of, in near optimal conditions. Bathed in extracellular fluid, cells receive food, water and oxygen and their wastes are disposed of. [24]

If a colony of cells is to work effectively as an organism, the activities of the different cells must be organised into a system. This requires *communication* between the cells. Within trees communication between cells is facilitated by a system of hormones that influence cell division, growth and differentiation. There are five hormones that are a medium of communication between cells in trees – the auxins, the gibberellins, abscicic acid, the cytokinins and ethylene. Auxins promote cell growth. Gibberellins break the dormancy of seeds. Abscicic acid suppresses cell division and expansion, whereas cytokinins prompt cells to divide. Different hormones function in different ways in different contexts. Hormones affect cells by interacting with receptors on the cell's surface. These receptors link up with secondary messengers within the cell, which transmit the message to specific parts of the cell. In addition, different hormones work together in pairs or groups. They have different effects in combination. [25]

Cells

Cells, such as plant cells, are organised for a purpose. The purpose of a cell – the basic unit of life – is, in common with multicellular organisms, to survive and reproduce.

Most cells are so small they are invisible to the naked eye. Plant cells generally vary in length from 10-100 micrometres – a micrometer is one ten thousandth of a centimetre. Some bacterial cells are only half a micrometre in length. [26] Despite their tiny size, a cell is extraordinarily complex. Plant cells have at least a dozen different types of specialised units (organelles) that are the analogues of organs (such as leaves, roots and flowers) in multicellular organisms. The parts work together – cooperate - to achieve the purposes of the whole of which they are a part, such as the survival and reproduction of the cell, and at the same time, their own survival and reproduction. Cells are thus collective survival and reproduction enterprises.

A typical plant cell consists of a cell membrane which encloses the cell fluid. The cell membrane is a cell boundary. It serves to enclose the network of vital processes of the cell, yet it participates in the network by selecting nutrients through special filters and disposing of waste. Suspended in the cell fluid are a number of specialised organelles. These structures work together and communicate with one another to enable a cell to maintain and reproduce itself. These include:

1. An information centre – this contains the genetic material in the form of nucleic acids – consisting of a set of templates for producing proteins needed for

> survival and reproduction. It also stores hereditary information that is passed from cell to cell as new cells are formed
> 2. recycling centres
> 3. energy centres
> 4. solar panels
> 5. production centres
> 6. a transport and communication centre. [27]

The solar panels or *chloroplasts* are organelles that carry out photosynthesis that converts light energy from the sun into chemical energy, in the form of sugars, using special pigment (chlorophyll) to capture light energy.

The sugars produced by the solar panels then travel to the cell's energy centres – the *mitochondria*. They take energy from food and convert it into a chemical energy carrier called *Adenosine Triphosphate* (ATP). They use oxygen to break down organic molecules into carbon dioxide and water. This releases energy that is locked up in ATP. These energy carriers travel to other part of the cell to supply energy necessary for vital processes.

The production centres – *ribosomes* – are the granular bodies in which the cell's proteins are produced. They consist of structural proteins, ribonucleic acids (RNA) as well as various enzymes – catalysts that facilitate the chemical processes of the cell.

The recycling centres contain enzymes for breaking down food, damaged cell components and unused molecules. These materials are then reused for building new cell components.

The transport and communication centre is a network of sacs and tubes that form channels through the cell fluid. It is also a site for the synthesis of enzymes involved in cellular respiration and is the primary site of membrane synthesis within a cell.

Cells are tiny colonies of macromolecules – such as proteins and nucleic acids. The life of a cell depends on a combination of labour between nucleic acids and proteins. Life is not a magic molecule. The magic lies in the relationship between molecules. The functioning of living cells is analogous to the functioning of a CD player. A CD player has two main components, hardware and software. Software, such as a CD, embodies information. Hardware processes that information. Living cells have hardware and software. A cell's hardware is mainly protein and its software is mainly nucleic acid. [28] There is a combination of labour within each living cell between nucleic acids (DNA and RNA) that store and transmit information and proteins that are catalysts to chemical reactions and form much of the structure of the cell. The proteins that make up most of a living body are produced inside cells in the ribosomes. DNA molecules serve as "templates" for the production of proteins. A particular sequence of DNA codes for a particular protein. To produce a protein, the relevant DNA sequence must be read by the cellular hardware (the proteins) just as the hardware of the CD player reads the CD in playing music. [29]

(The analogy between nucleic acids and software can only be stretched so far. Ribonucleic acids are part of the structure of, and so form the hardware of, ribosomes. Also, proteins can embody information. Recall the dual inheritance mechanisms of cells. Each cell has a dual inheritance system. One depends on copying genetic material and transmitting this to the next generation. The other involves copying and transmitting a state of gene activation. The latter inheritance mechanism is mediated by proteins but by definition it involves information transfer.)

Cell function also depends on a combination of labour within a cell between three distinct forms of ribonucleic acid (RNA). *Ribosomal* RNA is a structural component of the ribosomes. It places the amino acids (the building blocks of proteins) in the right order. *Transfer* RNA brings amino acids to the ribosome to be incorporated into proteins. *Messenger* RNA conveys genetic information from DNA to the ribosome. [30]

Cooperation and specialization produces synergies. Consider, for example, mitochondria. Today, it is generally accepted that mitochondria are descendents of formerly free living bacteria. It is hypothesized that millions of years ago small, free-living bacteria were engulfed, but not digested, by larger bacteria. Over time, the two organisms developed a symbiotic relationship, the larger organism providing the smaller with nutrients and safe lodgings, and the smaller organism providing the larger one with ATP molecules. Both partners benefited. [31]

Cooperation produces synergies, but it also creates interdependence and an individual stake in those synergies. The once independent mitochondria and chloroplasts still reproduce themselves separately from their host cells, utilising their own DNA. However, they depend entirely on materials as well as protection supplied by their hosts; they cannot exist independently.

Combinations of labour depend on communication and the different organelles that make up a cell communicate with each other (via the transport and communication centre). The macromolecular components of cells – proteins and nucleic acids – also have a sophisticated means of communication with each other. This communication is mediated by the *genetic code.* The association between DNA sequences and amino acids that make up proteins is called the genetic code. DNA molecules are built from four different chemicals – adenine, guanine, cytosine and thiamine. These chemicals form the "alphabet" of the language in which genetic information is stored. The four bases can be arranged in 64 permutations of three that code for the 20 amino acids that make up proteins. The genetic code is common to all life (with a few minor variations).

Superorganisms

Superorganisms are complex societies of organisms. Examples include colonies of social insects such as ants, termites and bees. Superorganisms are organised for a purpose. These societies are characterised by an extensive combination of labour between member organisms, that is, a specialisation of tasks and sub-tasks between colony members such as foraging, transport, defence of the colony, nest making, caring for the brood and reproduction. Each role corresponds to a functional part.

Leaf cutter ants make a living through agriculture. They grow an edible fungus in underground chambers of their nests. The fungus is grown on pellets made from leaves. Leaf cutter ants have developed a complex process for cultivating this fungus. It involves at least five broad tasks: cutting the leaves; transporting the leaf fragments to the nest; transforming the leaf fragments into pellets on which to grow the fungus; care of the underground gardens; and harvesting.

The process begins with a group of ants climbing trees, cutting away pieces of leaves with their sharp mandibles and allowing them to drop to the ground. Another group find the pieces, cut them into smaller pieces and carry them to a 'road' where a third group transports the leaf fragments back to the nest. These 'roads' may be 100 metres long. The ground along these roads is cleared for ease of transport. The foragers finally deposit the leaf pieces onto the floor of a nest chamber. Next the leaf fragments are stripped of their waxy outer layer, shredded and pulped. The resulting moist pellets are piled up in the chamber and inoculated with the edible fungus. The fungus gardens are tended carefully and ceaselessly. They are weeded of alien fungal spores. If necessary, fungus will be transported so that it can grow in optimal conditions. The fungus is also pruned to encourage growth. The garden is fertilised with ant manure, and treated with 'herbicides' - anti pathogens excreted by the ants that inhibit the growth of unwanted bacteria and fungi. When the harvest is ready, the fungus is cropped – the knob-like end of the fungus is removed. [32]

The different tasks in this process are allocated to different 'castes' based on their size. Foragers – about the size of house flies - cut leaves and transport them to the nest. Smaller ants cut the leaves into smaller fragments, and smaller ants again crush and mould the fragments into pellets, and the very smallest ants – the minima – tend the garden. [33]

Whether a leaf cutter ant is a queen, a soldier, a forager or minima is unlikely to depend on different genes, but arises from the response of a similar genotype to different social circumstances. The different "castes" of a leaf cutter ant colony are likely to be induced by different diets, at any rate different chemical signals, to develop in different ways according to the needs of the colony.

Tasks relating to the defence of colony are also allocated according to size. Protection against enemy insects is allocated to the soldiers – 300 times heavier than the minima and about 2 centimetres in length. [34] But minima also have a role in the defence of the colony. They sometimes travel outside the nest where they patrol edges of trails watching for danger and issuing alarms. They ride on leaf fragments to defend from attack by parasitoid flies. [35]

The role of the queen is to establish the new colony, including its first fungus garden, and raise the first group of about 20 workers. For the rest of her life she becomes an egg-laying machine. Mature leaf cutter colonies are enormous, consisting of up to 8 million ants. [36] The queen lays all the eggs. Reproductive labour is devolved to the queen, though her workers will tend the larvae.

Leaf cutter ant colonies – in common with all social insect colonies – are collective survival and reproduction enterprises. Colony members work together to collectively achieve the purposes of the colony – to survive and reproduce – but also to meet the needs of each colony member. This is achieved through a combination of labour. Survival and reproduction requires work. A solitary insect must carry out all the tasks associated with survival and reproduction – such as gathering, preparing and consuming food and water, disposing of waste, controlling temperature, defending against potential predators, perhaps constructing a home, finding a mate, mating, caring for the young – largely on its own, or with a mate. So a solitary insect tends to be a jack of all trades but a master of none. In an insect colony, members undertake all of these tasks collectively. But not all members do all of these tasks. They specialise. For instance, the queen specialises in reproductive labour. She establishes a new nest and lays all the eggs that will hatch into ant larvae and eventually colony members. (Some insect colonies have multiple queens, but many have a single queen). All of the queen's daughters are sterile. They cannot reproduce. Male ants are produced from unfertilised eggs. Their only role in the colony is to mate with fertile females – potential new queens for new colonies. We have seen that depending on their size, some leaf cutter ants specialise in cutting leaves, others in transporting them to the nest, others again in processing the leaves. The smallest ants tend the underground fungus gardens. The largest ants – the soldiers – specialise in protection of the colony – though the minima do some protective labour as well. Other ants are tunnelling specialists and older ants waste disposal specialists. All this labour is combined into an organised system.

The net effect is that collectively the colony can do what no solitary ant can do. Collectively, an ant colony is a master of all trades associated with survival and reproduction. All of the tasks necessary to survival and reproduction can be carried out collectively at the same time. Workers can specialise in one role, and do it well, without being distracted by the need to attend to a myriad of other tasks.

The ants in a leaf cutter ant colony depend on each other for their survival. A leaf cutter ant could not survive for long if isolated from its colony.

In order for the colony to work effectively – for specialisation of labour to be an organised system rather than a chaotic one – requires effective *communication* between colony members. Communication is a requisite for any cooperation in living systems. It requires information to be transferred from one individual to another - accurately. In ant colonies communication is based on secretions of chemicals called pheromones that are passed back and forth between the ants to be tasted and smelled. [37] This chemically based communication system is supplemented (or nuanced) by bodily movements, by touching, regurgitation and by sound. [38] Communication requires that different combinations of pheromones code for something that individual ants can decode in the same way and act appropriately. It is estimated that ants use between 10 and 20 chemical "words" and "phrases" each having a distinct meanings associated with attraction, recruitment, alarm and so on. [39] The mix of 'castes' produced in a colony is also regulated by excretions from the queen and soldiers in accordance with the needs of the colony. [40]

Another condition for the effective functioning of a superorganism would appear to be sharing. Sharing of food and water tightens social bonds. Processes of sharing underpin social life amongst social insects. [41] Most ant species store food and water in their bodies in an organ called "the crop". In many ant species colony members beg for food by touching the mouth of a food bearer, who immediately regurgitates liquid from their crop. [42] Portions of liquefied food, radioactively labelled, introduced to a colony of common black ants by a single worker reach every other worker in the colony within a day – through reciprocal feeding. Within a week all colony members carry approximately the same amount of the radioactive material. This suggests that at any moment the amount one colony member holds in her crop is likely to be the same as every other member. So when one ant is hungry they all are – to about the same degree. This conveys valuable information to colony members. When the colony requires a particular nutrient, the foragers require it too and so seek it without having to be directed by a central command. When everyone has roughly the same stomach content individual decisions are more harmonised with the collective needs. Thus the crop serves as a "social stomach" for the colony. [43]

Ecosystems

An ecosystem can be defined as a biological community and the physical environment associated with it. [44] Examples of ecosystems include rain forests and coral reefs. I would define 'ecosystem' more narrowly as a system of inter-related species or lineages of organisms.

Ecosystems are organised for a purpose. One purpose of an ecosystem is to recycle the materials necessary for life. Some of the materials necessary to construct living organisms are in relatively short supply. Cycling of these materials by ecosystems is a critical part of the life support system of the planet. [45] The purpose of an ecosystem is different from a cell, an organism or a superorganism. Ecosystems are collective *recycling* enterprises. The components of an ecosystem work together to recycle those elements necessary for life.

An ecosystem is made up of two subsystems. There is an open energy subsystem and a more or less closed cyclical materials subsystem. The function of the energy subsystem is to power the operation of the ecosystem. The function of the materials subsystem is to provide the necessary molecules required for the components of the ecosystem. [46] Together the two subsystems provide for the continuing functioning of the ecosystem.

An ecosystem is made up of different functional parts, such as:

1. primary producers – that produce their own food
2. herbivores – that consume primary producers
3. carnivores – that consume herbivores or other carnivores
4. omnivores – that consume primary producers and carnivores and/or herbivores
5. detritivores – that consume dead bodies and waste products of other organisms. [47]

Chemical elements and compounds are transferred from organism to organism through food webs. Chemicals necessary for life are transferred from primary producers, to herbivores, to carnivores and omnivores. As these organisms die, and as they produce waste, their bodies/wastes are consumed by detritivores that break these down to produce chemicals that in turn are taken up by primary producers.

For example, in a South American tropical rainforest the primary producers include trees, epiphytes and lianas. A few herbivores (such as Howler Monkeys) feed off the leaves but most herbivores consume seeds, fruit and nectar that are easier to digest and contain fewer if any chemical defences. Carnivores include jaguars, ocelots, harpy eagles and anacondas. In tropical rainforests a large source of food for detritivores is leaf litter. As leaf litter decomposes nutrients contained within it enter the soil for uptake to vegetation. A mutualistic relationship (that is, one in which both species benefit) between trees and fungi ensure that nutrients released through decomposition are rapidly adsorbed by trees. [48]

Relationships between members of different species within an ecosystem are not generally competitive. Members of different species tend to avoid competition with each other by occupying distinct niches within an ecosystem – that is, distinct ways of making a living. Resources tend to be *shared* by dividing up resources, through specialisation, allowing exploitation by different components of resources by different species. This process is called *resource partitioning*.

For example, common European shorebirds all feed in similar muddy areas and appear to occupy the same niche. Their bills, however, are of a different length, and thus the birds exploit different components of animals in the sediment. Thus members of these different species of bird occupy distinct niches and so do not compete with each other. [49]

Another example of resource partitioning involves the large *herbivorous* mammals grazing the Serengeti plains in Tanzania, Africa. Giraffes share the same habitat with impala and buffalo, but because giraffes obtain their food from the tops of trees they do not compete for food with the impala that utilise vegetation closer to the ground. [50] Nor do they compete for food with grass eating herbivores such as wildebeest. Small herbivores eat high quality food such as shoots and flowers. Larger animals feed on more abundant grass. Thus small and large herbivores do not compete for food.

Competition between different species of *carnivore* in the Serengeti is avoided by resource partitioning. For example, the four main carnivores of the Serengeti eat slightly different prey, hunt at different times and employ different hunting techniques. [51]

Many tropical forest herbivores are restricted to feeding on just a few species. Some live on the ground, others in both trees and on the ground and others in trees only. Some feed during the day, others at night only and some during day and night. Thus the herbivores are not generally in competition with each other. [52] The abundance of fruits, seeds, buds, nectar and insects in rainforests has allowed birds to become specialist feeders and thus avoid competition with each other.

Generally speaking species tend to co-evolve away from competition with each other. Rather than compete within a single niche, two species may co-evolve to occupy two distinct niches in which they are not in competition. Competition is generally harmful to living systems – at least their lives are better without it - and if it can be avoided it will be.

Ecosystems are not superorganisms. The members of a superorganism are functionally interdependent. Each 'caste' depends on every other 'caste' carrying out their functions for their survival. For example, all colony members of a leaf cutter ant society depend on specialised foragers, soldiers, nurses, and gardeners for their survival. But, while some relationships within an ecosystem are mutualistic, many of the direct dependency relationships between living systems within an ecosystem are one way – down the food chain.

Herbivores are dependent on primary producers for their food and survival, but primary producers are not directly dependent on herbivores for their survival. Similarly, primary carnivores are directly dependent on herbivores and indirectly dependent on the primary producers for their survival – but neither herbivores nor primary producers are directly dependent on carnivores for their survival.

Indeed members of prey species have an obvious interest in not being preyed upon. Thus prey species evolve defences against predation and predator species evolve improved techniques for prey capture. These improvements in predation and defence tend to keep step with each other – so an improvement in predatory skills of a predator will be matched by an improvement in the prey species' defence. Paradoxically, if a predator species were to gain the upper hand over its prey the predator species may force the prey species, and so in turn itself, into extinction. If a prey species were to gain the upper hand over its predators, this could result in a population explosion in the prey species and increased competition between members of the prey species for increasingly scarce resources. This might pose a threat to the sustainability of the prey species.

At least indirectly, however, producers do depend on consumers for their survival and reproduction. For example, most trees (producers) directly depend on a mutualistic relationship with the fungi (consumers) that infiltrate their roots. The fungi gain because they take sugars from the tree. The tree gains because the fungi are functional extensions of their roots and increase their efficiency and their effective absorptive area. Being heterotrophs, fungi live by breaking down organic material and the trees benefit from the nutrients released by this process. Many species of tree benefit from close cooperation (via root nodules) with heterotrophic nitrogen-fixing bacteria. Detritivores (consumers) break down materials to forms that can be reassimilated by producers. Most land plants could not survive without soil – but soil is produced largely by detritivores.

Carnivores and herbivores greatly increase the speed and efficiency of recycling nutrients. Carnivores and herbivores can carry nutrients in their bodies quickly and often over vast distances. These nutrients are eventually returned to producers via waste products and eventually consumption of their bodies by decomposers. The bodies of heterotrophs are in effect a compost heap for what they eat.

While an ecosystem is not an organism or superorganism it is organised for a purpose. The components of an ecosystem – species – work together, co-operate, to recycle the materials necessary to sustain life. Such recycling and its benefits to living systems could not be achieved without cooperation between producers and consumers. Species within an ecosystem avoid competition by sharing or partitioning resources. The component species in an ecosystem depend on each other for recycling services – something a species cannot accomplish on its own.

Harmony: At the core of life?

It might be objected that my claim that the basic process of life is the process of cooperation and harmony confuses outcome with process. While the outcome of natural selection may be harmonious, the process of natural selection is competitive.

The great Japanese scientist Kinji Imanishi observed that harmony is at the core of life. He argued that different but related species select their own lifestyles and micro habitats, which allows them to co-exist harmoniously in the same environment.

In his excellent book, *The Ape and the Sushi Master* Dutch primatologist Frans de Waal replies to this claim that "if two related organisms live peacefully side by side in different ecological niches, this does not necessarily mean that their initial parting of the ways wasn't based on competition." [53]

De Waal claims that to "depict nature as harmonious, as Iminishi did, is entirely legitimate, there are indeed large segments characterised by peaceful co-existence, equilibrium, and symbiosis. To look for competition is equally legitimate, and such an enterprise doesn't come up empty-handed either." [54]

De Waal claims that Imanishi confuses process and outcome. He writes "Even though the process of natural selection is inherently competitive, it has produced all sorts of tendencies and configurations in nature, including socially positive and cooperative ones... Inasmuch as confusion between process and outcome has led scientists in the West to doubt that humans and animals can be genuinely nice, we shouldn't be too hard on Imanishi for making the opposite error, which was that he doubted the competitive nature of evolution because of the harmony he felt it had produced." [55]

Evolution without competition

It is a widespread dogma of biology that competition is the basis of natural selection and evolution. David Dusenbery writes that "micro-organisms have evolved a diversity of behaviours to aid in the *competition* among life forms that is at the foundation of evolution by natural selection." [56]

Steve Jones claims "Life is a struggle. As more individuals are born than can possibly survive, a grain in the balance will determine which individual shall live and which shall die. The slightest *advantage* in any one being, at any age or during any season, over those which it comes into *competition*, will turn the balance. Natural selection is simple. It picks up inherited differences in the capacity to reproduce. If one version multiplies itself *better than others* it will take over and, in the end, a new form of life – a new species – will emerge." (Emphasis added) [57]

The idea that competition forms the basis of natural selection goes back at least as far a Charles Darwin's classic *The Origin of Species*. The book is sub-titled "By means of natural selection or the preservation of favoured races in the struggle for life." Darwin explains natural selection as follows.

> Can it, then, be thought improbable ... that ... variations useful in some way to each being in the great struggle for life should occur in the course of many successive generations? If such do occur, can we doubt (remembering that many more individuals are born than can survive) that individuals having any *advantage, however slight, over others* would have the best chance of surviving and procreating their own? (Emphasis added) [58]

Thus formulated, competition is necessary to natural selection. Elsewhere in *Origin* Darwin gives a slightly different account of natural selection.

> Natural selection acts exclusively by the preservation and accumulation of variations, which

are *beneficial* under the organic and inorganic conditions of life to which each creature is exposed at all periods of life. (Emphasis added) [59]

It may metaphorically be said that natural selection is daily and hourly scrutinizing, throughout the world, the slightest variations; rejecting those that are *bad*, preserving and adding up all that are *good*; silently and insensibly working, *whenever and wherever opportunity offers*, at the improvement of each organic being in relation to its organic and inorganic conditions of life. (Emphasis added)[60]

On this account of natural selection, variations that are beneficial to an organism are preserved and those that are harmful are eliminated. No reference is made in this account to *advantage* over others. Nor is any reference made to competition. On this account, competition is not necessary to natural selection. In other words, natural selection is not inherently competitive.

It might be thought that any benefit to an organism is also an advantage. But consider an imaginary example. Suppose a cassowary mutates in a manner that allows it to eat a blue rainforest fruit that its fellows cannot. Its fellows eat red fruit. Suppose that the blue fruit is plentiful and highly nutritious. Then chances are the trait will be passed on to succeeding generations. A number of scenarios are possible.

1. Blue Fruit becomes common but red fruit becomes scarce. Cassowaries that eat blue fruit flourish while those that eat red fruit die out. (Jones' scenario)

2. Blue fruit is common but so is red fruit. The two varieties of cassowary (red-fruit and blue-fruit-eating varieties) live side by side.
3. Blue fruit is common on the plains. Red fruit is common on the slopes. The blue fruit cassowaries become common on the plains and the red fruit cassowaries become common on the slopes. The two varieties become geographically isolated.

Each scenario involves natural selection. But only the first involves a struggle for existence. Competition for available food resources can drive natural selection, but competition or the struggle for existence is not necessary for natural selection. Natural selection preserves all beneficial traits not only those that confer a competitive advantage.

Imanishi claims that when one species evolves into another, the species *en masse* adopts a different life style. This is similar to the second and third scenarios above. Mutations may indeed lead a species to adopt a different life style, rather than being forced into this lifestyle change by competition.

Mutations may result in organisms developing new "preferences". For example, lichen might mutate in such a way that it can tolerate or even prefer sunnier conditions than its ancestors. Another may mutate in a way that it can tolerate, or even prefer shadier conditions than its ancestors. (When I speak of lichen having a preference for shade, I am not meaning to suggest that they have a desire for shade, but rather, they flourish in shady conditions.) The differentially mutated lichens might colonise different parts of a rock face depending on the angle of the rock face and the amount of direct sunlight shining on the rock. One type of lichen may "choose" or "select" a sunny part of the rock face according to its preference, and another may "choose" or "select" a shady part according to its preference. A great deal of natural selection may work in this way.

Living systems and mechanical systems

Living systems in common with human artifacts are organised for a purpose. It is entirely natural to ask of an artifact – an object made by an intelligent designer – What is its purpose? What are the functions of its parts? What problems does it solve? [61] It seems equally natural to ask these questions of a living system. In this respect, a living system would appear to be analogous to an artifact.

But how close is the analogy? Darwin, after all, taught us that living systems are not artifacts - they are not made by an intelligent designer. Could the artifact model [62] of living systems be a vestige of natural theology? Physicists do not invoke purposes. Is this because Biology is behind the times? Have biologists been unable to free themselves from the historical roots of their discipline in natural theology? Or does it reflect a real difference in the nature of the subject matter of Biology compared to Physics? Perhaps it reflects the fact that Biology is the study of complex things, whereas Physics is the study of simple things that do not tempt us to invoke design? [63]

Living systems, as we have seen, are analogous to mechanical systems in a number of respects. Living systems, in common with mechanical systems have functional parts and purposes, they are organised – the parts of the system work together to achieve the purposes of the whole. There appear, however, to be significant differences between mechanical systems and living systems.

Mechanical systems derive their complexity and purpose from their human designers and makers. For example, a ship might serve as a mode of transport, as a floating restaurant moored in a harbour, or be sunk and used as an artificial reef. Whatever purpose the ship might have – as transport, restaurant or reef - depends on the use humans or other living systems make of it. Mechanical systems never have their own ends or purposes. They are designed to serve human purposes. The purposes of mechanical systems, then, are *extrinsic* or external to the system.

Not so living systems. Living systems do not derive their complexity and purpose from their designers or makers. *Living systems have their own ends or purposes*, such as survival and reproduction. That is, some of the purposes of living systems are *intrinsic* or internal to the system. Living systems have some extrinsic purposes. For example, cats eat mice. A mouse, then, may have an *extrinsic* purpose as food for a cat. But the mouse has its own intrinsic purposes, including evasion of furry predators.

Living systems are not machines, like watches, constructed and directed from outside by a divine watchmaker. [64] And nor are they machines created by their genes. [65] Living systems have ends of their own.

Any natural theology, especially a greener faith, [66] needs to address the apparent implication of the view of living systems as the product of a transcendent, disembodied sky god, [67] that living systems in common with human artifacts derive their purpose and value entirely from without. On such a view living systems, including human beings, literally are artifacts. They have no real value in themselves. This may pave the way for treating non-human living systems as we wish. It should not be too surprising then that some theologians wish to separate an understanding of divine providence from "the abstract – and rather lifeless – notion of a divine designer." [68] Other theologians, who do not wish to distinguish divine providence from design, still stress God's self-limitation - that "creation is allowed to be itself and make itself." [69]

Conferring purpose

Living systems, unlike artifacts, *confer* purpose or function on their parts.

Cells confer purpose

A cell confers purpose on its micro-molecular components. For example, we have seen that DNA is analogous to a compact disc. DNA is a passive molecule that does nothing outside the context of a cell, just as a CD does nothing outside of the context of a CD player. DNA codes for proteins, but the DNA just sits there while from time to time the cell reads from it a sequence to make a needed protein. [70]

A eukaryotic cell (a cell with a nucleus, and mitochondria) confers purpose on its mitochondria. Mitochondria can be fairly described as energy centres for a cell. Their free living ancestors could not be so described. The cell confers this function on its mitochondria.

Multicellular organisms confer purpose
Multicellular organisms confer purpose on its cells in the process of cell differentiation or specialisation. Human beings, for example, have many different kinds of cells with differing functions – nerve cells, liver cells, blood cells, muscle cells, skin cells and so on. Very early in the development of an embryo the cells are undifferentiated, but in a human embryo, by about the third day, differentiation begins.

Whether a human cell is a nerve cell, a liver cell, a blood cell or a muscle cell – that is, the function of a cell - is not determined by differences in the genes the cell carries, for all of the cells in a multicellular organism carry the same genes. Multicellular organisms begin their life as just a single cell, and the process of mitosis ensures that all the genes pass to all of the cells. So the genes in each cell of a multicellular organism are identical. As we have seen, differences in gene activation account for the differences between the functions of those cells. The genes switched on in a nerve cell differ from those switched on in a muscle cell or a blood cell.

Genes can be switched on or off by other molecules in a cell depending on the system's need for a particular protein. Fluctuations in the environment of a cell influence whether a particular gene is switched on or off.

For example, bacteria in a glucose rich environment do not produce enzymes necessary to metabolise the sugar lactose. If the diet of these bacteria is restricted to lactose only, the bacteria produce a lactose enzyme. These bacteria already have the DNA sequences necessary to produce a lactose enzyme, but it is switched off in glucose rich environments and switched on in lactose rich environments. The bacteria's interaction with its environment determines whether the gene is switched on or off. [71]

Some of the molecules that turn genes on or off are produced in the same cell. In multicellular organisms, molecules such as hormones, produced in one cell may penetrate the membrane and the nucleus of a cell in a different part of the body and switch a gene on or off. [72]

In multicellular organisms, each cell's nucleus is inundated with chemical signals arriving from all directions. A gene-inhibiting molecule may arrive at the same time as a gene-activating molecule. The two may interact or compete in ways that allow for differing degrees of gene activation. [73]

Such mechanisms ensure genes are switched on only when and where the gene's product is needed by the organism for maintaining its own good health. Living wholes turn on or off their genes according to the needs of the system. They thus confer purpose on their genes.

Multicellular organisms confer purpose on their macromolecular components. In a human being, for example, the protein Keratin has a structural function in making hair and nails. Fibrin is used for blood clotting.

Insulin is used to control blood glucose levels and Oxytocin used to regulate milk production. Actin and Myosin regulate contraction of muscle fibres and antibodies mark foreign proteins for elimination. They would not have these functions outside the context of a body. [74]

Multicellular organisms confer purpose on their tissues and organs in a similar way that cells confer purpose on their organelles.

Superorganisms confer purpose
Superorganisms confer purpose or function on their components – in a way that resembles cell differentiation. In some superorganisms, the component organisms are morphologically similar, and may switch tasks according to the colony's needs. In such cases individuals switch tasks partly in response to environmental cues. But environmental cues are not enough – individuals must communicate with each other. Work is organised by local communication between individuals – such as the figure eight dance of the honey bee that indicates the distance and direction of a food source, or the chemical communication between ants. Global order – that is, task allocation according to the needs of the colony – results from application of local rules. [75]

In other cases – such as the leafcutter ants – there is a morphological difference between the members of the colony, such as a difference in size. While individuals from different castes are genetically similar, during their development they are exposed to different diets and different chemical signals, that contributes to different morphologies. [76]

In either event the whole (the colony) confers function or purpose on the parts (individuals).

Ecosystems confer purpose

We have seen that ecosystems generate niches or employment opportunities for lineages. In the context of a particular ecosystem, species function as primary producers, consumers or decomposers. Ecosystems generate more specific niches as well. The ecosystem, then, confers purpose on its constituent living components.

Conferring purpose is a form of causation. Genetic determinists would argue that the parts of an organism determine the traits of the organism. Causation flows from the part (genes) to the whole (organism) in one direction – via proteins, cells, tissues, and organs. But if organisms confer purpose on their organs, cells and macromolecular components such as DNA, then causation can also flow from the whole to the part – that is, downward causation. The fact that living systems confer purpose on their components is incompatible with both reductionism and genetic determinism that would insist only on upward causation.

Organisation and evolution

In *The Origins of Life* John Maynard Smith and Eors Szathmary define as "living" any population of entities possessing properties necessary to evolve by natural selection. These properties include:

- multiplication – that is, each entity can produce two or more similar entities
- variation – that is, although they are similar they are not identical
- heredity – that is, like entities beget like. The occasional breakdown of heredity gives rise to variation. [77]

Maynard Smith and Szathmary note that continuing evolution requires unlimited heredity, in which an indefinitely large number of structures are each capable of replication. [78]

I would suggest that more fundamental properties need to be possessed by entities if they are to evolve by natural selection. First, in order to be capable of heredity, especially unlimited heredity, an entity must be organised. Unlimited heredity requires that the parts of an entity work together as an organised whole to produce two or more similar entities. In life as we know it, unlimited heredity requires the cooperation (in fact a combination of labour) between nucleic acids and proteins.

This implies that organisation in life does not arise solely from evolution by natural selection. So how else could it arise? Some possibilities include:

- intelligent design – though intelligent behaviour appears to presuppose organisation too, say of a brain, or a body. Even a disembodied intelligence would seem to require some organisation

- self-organisation – J Scott Turner argues that "organisms are designed [organised] not so much because of natural selection of particular genes has made them that way, but because agents of homeostasis have made them that way" [79]
- building on organisation in non-living systems. Non-living systems may be organised – though not necessarily for a purpose. There are many examples of synergy – an effect of cooperation – in the non-living world. One example is a vortex in a bath when the plug is pulled out. This is produced by the combination of different forces – gravity, water pressure, air pressure, centrifugal forces and the properties of water. Another example is the combination of chlorine and sodium to produce a totally new substance – table salt. [80]

Purpose and evolution

Evolution by natural selection presupposes organisation for a purpose. A population of entities not to some degree bent on staying alive would not survive much less reproduce, and so would not evolve by natural selection. Teleology then is not, as is sometimes claimed, purely a product of evolution. Evolution by natural selection *presupposes purpose.*

Imagine a population of entities with properties of multiplication, variation and heredity living on an Earth-like planet. Imagine that these entities varied in the degree to which they were bent on living, living well and living better. Now wind the clock forward 4 billion years. The descendants of this population would likely, to a very high degree, to be motivated to live, live well and live better for such entities are more likely to survive and reproduce their kind than entities that are less motivated to do so.

This suggests that living systems are organised for purposes other than mere survival and reproduction.

Living involves simply staving off death.

Living well involves maintaining good health (including healthy development). A single celled organism, for example an amoeba, is not merely alive but *bent on staying alive.* The tiny organism strives to keep the chemical profile of its internal milieu in balance (maintain good health) while external to the system all hell may be breaking loose. [81] Living systems are organised for optimal health – that is, they are organised in such a way that they are good enough to do the job adequately in most circumstances. Just as lift cables have a safety factor built into them – they are 12 times as strong as they need to be in relation to the maximum load imposed in normal use – living systems also have safety factors built into them. The silk of a spider has a safety factor of 1.5 and the leg bone of a kangaroo has a safety factor of 3. Such margins of safety are a compromise between strength and many other vital functions. Increases in safety factors are energetically expensive, and with limited resources may not be worth the investment. [82]

Living better involves improving the quality of one's life by making the process of living easier and more efficient. Making a living is hard work and living systems strive to make it easier and more efficient – often by cooperating with other living systems.

It is sometimes claimed that living systems are organised to reproduce. This is not true of all living systems. Single celled organisms reproduce in the most straight forward way – by mitotic division – a "parent" cell becomes two "daughters". In sexually reproducing beings individual organisms do not reproduce by themselves. In sexually reproducing organisms, males and females work together to continue their lineage. The offspring are equally the male and the females. Many social insects outsource reproduction to specialists (specifically "the queen"). All living organisms, however, are organised to contribute to the reproductive process.

Rather than say that living systems are organised to survive and reproduce, it is more accurate say that they are organised to live, live well, live better and contribute to the process of reproduction – the continuation of their lineage.

That the purposefulness of living systems is a requisite for evolution by natural selection can be seen by considering a slightly different account of the conditions for evolution. Simon Conway Morris cites four basic rules for the game of life, but more accurately they are rules for the emergence of evolutionary trends and complexity. The rules are:

1. Hindsight and foresight are strictly forbidden.
2. Minor changes are easier than major changes.
3. Resources are not unlimited: the world is finite, and ultimately energy and space are restricted in supply.
4. Life has no option but to carry on; it must always play the best hand it can no matter how poor or

disastrous the hand might be and no matter who or what offers the challenge. [83]

Symbioses and sex are two good ways to speed up the game. [84] Conway Morris suggests that one evolutionary trend not explained by these rules is morphological convergence – such as the development of similar eyes in squids and humans, or the development of agriculture in leaf-cutter ants and humans. [85]

I believe that morphological convergence could be explained by these rules, depending on how we interpret the rule that life must always play the best hand it can, no matter how poor that hand might be. If the hand dealt to life is just a series of problems thrown up by an environment that is hostile or at best indifferent to it, then morphological convergence cannot be explained by the four rules. If, however, the hand dealt to life includes a genetic and social tool kit; an inheritance for solving problems and exploiting opportunities, refined over billions of years, and if that tool kit includes only a limited number of tools that can be drawn on (or not) as the need arises, then the fact that different lines of life "invent" similar solutions to similar problems is not so surprising.

The main point I wish to make is that rule 4 implies an internal teleology or purpose. For in what sense does life have *no option* but to carry on? It is conceivable, logically and empirically, though it is unlikely, that life on Earth could be destroyed say by a collision with an asteroid or comet. The Earth itself will one day be destroyed by an expanding sun. It is also conceivable that life could destroy itself. Humans may some day have the capability if not the will to destroy life on Earth.

One sense in which life has no option but to carry on is that living systems have a will or a purpose to live, live well and live better and contribute to reproducing their kind. Some, whose life is full of suffering, may lose the will to live. But few living systems do.

Purpose and desire

Purposes are not the same as desires. Purposes and desires share a number of features in common. They are both motivators of their bearers and ends or goals of a system. However, there are differences.

- Purposes are *universal* to all living systems. Not all living systems have desires.
- Purposes are *intrinsic* to living systems - built into their bodies. Desires are not built into bodies in the same way - they come and they go.
- Purposes are *objective* features of living systems – their existence does not depend on a conscious subject. Desires are subjective – they could not exist without a conscious subject.
- Purposes are *innate*, they are inherited genetically. In general, desires are acquired.
- Purposes are rather *limited* - to survival, reproduction and good health. What can be desired or wanted is unlimited. Humans, in particular, are capable of wanting or desiring just about anything.

All living systems are organised for intrinsic purposes. There is a close conceptual connection between purpose and value. Anything that is good (valuable) is good *for* something (purposeful). Functional ends or goals constitute norms with respect to which a means chosen may be judged good or bad. This suggests we may be able to move from saying that all living systems have intrinsic purpose to saying that all living systems have intrinsic value. In the next Chapter I will examine whether living systems are intrinsically valuable, and if so, in what sense.

Chapter Two: Value

The history of western ethics has revolved around a debate between two views about the source and nature of value (by which I mean good, bad, right, wrong, beauty and ugliness). According to the humanist view, the source of all value is humanity – value is rooted in human nature, the human condition or human desires. The other view is transcendental. It locates the source of value outside the human realm in a transcendent source that imposes on humanity the requirement to aspire to ends located beyond the physical world, commonly in a life after death. [86] The great ethical debate that has confronted western thinkers, and still does, is that between a fundamentally humanistic view and the transcendent view of the source of value it opposes. [87]

In this chapter I suggest that the debate should be broadened to consider a third view about the source of value - that value springs from life, not just human life or a transcendent realm. This has implications for answering one of the most significant questions any individual can ask "how shall I live in order to live a good life?" [88] One possible answer to this question is "Respectfully of all living things." (See Chapter Three)

Life as thick with value

It is clear from reading Charles Darwin's *The Origin of Species* that he thought that the living world was thick with purpose and value. In Chapter Four of *The Origin of Species*, on Natural Selection, Darwin's language for describing living processes and what he calls "organic beings" is rich in teleological and value terms.

Darwin characterises natural selection in terms of the *interests* of organic beings. He states that Natural Selection "...implies only the preservation of such variations as arise and are *beneficial* to the being under its conditions of life." [89] "Beneficial" means "anything that is for the good of a person or thing."

The use of value terms to define "natural selection" becomes explicit in later passages. "Man selects only for his own *good*: Nature only for that of the being which she tends." [90] "...natural selection is daily and hourly scrutinising, throughout the world, the slightest variations; rejecting those that are *bad*, preserving and adding up all that are *good*..."[91] "...natural selection can act only through and for the *good* of each being..." [92]

Darwin appears to be imputing to organic beings a means-end logic. The purposes or ends of living beings constitute standards (norms or values) relative to which certain means, or characters, may be judged good or bad.

Interestingly, Darwin also attributed beauty to organic beings and a sense of beauty to birds and other organisms. He writes "...if man can in short time *give beauty* and an elegant carriage to his bantams, according to his standard of beauty, I can see no good reason to doubt that female birds, by selecting, during thousands of generations, the most melodious or beautiful males according to their standard of beauty, might produce a marked effect." [93] "...if feeble man can do much by artificial selection, I can see no limit to the amount of change, to the *beauty* and complexity of the coadaptations between all organic beings..." [94]

The fact that Darwin appears to have believed that the living world is thick with purpose and value does not make it so. But Darwin appears to have had good reason to suppose that organic beings have purposes and values. For selection of variations or traits appears to involve selection in accordance with certain standards. Variations are artificially selected in accordance with human standards of beauty or utility. Sexual selection, say, of a peacock's vibrantly beautiful tail, is in accordance with the standards of beauty of the peahen – or generations of peahens. By analogy, a trait or variation is naturally selected in accordance with standards of whether that trait is good, (or favourable, or beneficial, or advantageous) for the being or its lineage. A heritable variation in the colour of a flower may be of no benefit to the individual plant, but may be highly beneficial to a lineage if the new colour is more attractive to particular and abundant pollinating insects or birds.

Darwin notes objections to the term "natural selection" "that it implies conscious choice in the animals which become modified; and it has been urged that, as plants have no volition, natural selection is not applicable to them." [95] But even artificial selection does not always imply conscious choice. Darwin distinguishes between methodical and unconscious means of artificial selection. He writes "In the case of methodical selection, a breeder selects for some definite object...But when many men, without intending to alter the breed, have a nearly common standard of perfection, and all try to procure and breed from the best animals, improvement surely but slowly follows from this unconscious process of selection." [96] Selection need not always involve conscious choice, but it must involve a standard or value relative to which the trait is selected.

While artificial and sexual selection implies a conscious or unconscious choice of a particular heritable trait, natural selection does not imply any choice, conscious or unconscious, on the part of Nature. Darwin writes "it is difficult to avoid personifying the word Nature; but I mean by Nature, only the aggregate action and product of many natural laws, and by laws the sequence of events as ascertained by us." [97] Nature, then, does not literally select anything – consciously or unconsciously. Nature is not an agent. Natural selection, however, does occur in accordance with standards or values. "Man selects only for his own good; Nature only for that of the being which she tends." [98]

Indeed according to Darwin, natural selection occurs relative to a higher standard than artificial selection. Darwin writes "How fleeting are the wishes and efforts of man! How short his time! And consequently how poor will be his results, compared with those accumulated by Nature during whole geological periods! Can we wonder, then, that Nature's productions should be far "truer" in character than man's productions; that they should be infinitely better adapted to the most complex conditions of life, and should plainly bear the stamp of far higher workmanship?" [99] Darwin is not suggesting here that Nature is an agent, but rather that the products of natural selection reflect a higher standard than the products of artificial selection.

"Natural selection" could be defined simply as the process by which some traits come to predominate in a population, while others decline in frequency. [100] This definition does appear to be value neutral but it is a bit uninformative. For in virtue of what do some traits come to predominate while others decline in frequency? One reply could be that some traits contribute to "superior fitness" where "fitness" is defined as a measure of the ability of a gene, organism or other biological unit to reproduce itself. [101] How would we measure this ability and the contribution a trait makes to it? We would need to take care not to measure it in terms of the predominance of the trait in a population – for that would lead to circularity. Or we could measure the contribution that the trait makes to the well being of its bearer, or lineage, and the impact this has on reproductive success. This would lead us back to Darwin's account.

Living systems as the source of value
There is a connection between purpose and value. Anything which is good is good for something. A purpose or an end constitutes a standard by which particular things are evaluated as good or bad, and certain courses of action right or wrong. So if I have an end to maintain good health, then resources contributing to that end, such as

good food, clean water, clean air, are valued means to achieving that end. Clean air is good for me relative to that end. Other things, such as toxins in my food and drinking water or in the air that I breathe are bad for me relative to that same end. If I have an end, then the means to achieve that end are valued. So purpose creates value – or more accurately, value and purpose are inter-linked, conceptually.

Conferring purpose and valuing are inseparable. If you confer purpose on something, then you value that thing and the means to achieve that end. If you value something, you value it as an end in itself or as a means to an end.

All living systems have ends. As we have seen, a living system is organised for a purpose. [102] A living system has specific ends, and the activity of the parts of the system is organised towards the achievement of those ends. The ends of a living system include survival – that is, staving off death [103] and maintaining good health.

But a living system values certain resources instrumentally as a means to achieve this basic good.

For example, a frangipanni, in common with all living systems, has specific ends for example, maintaining good health. To achieve this end, a frangipanni requires resources: oxygen, carbon dioxide, soil nutrients, sunshine and water. These resources are valuable for the frangipanni. They are valued instrumentally [104] by the plant as a means for achieving its ends.

So a frangipanni, in common with all living systems, is able to value. [105] It fundamentally values its own flourishing and instrumentally values whatever resources are necessary to flourish.

Thus all living systems are sources of value. All living systems have ends and ends generate value, so living systems generate, and are a source of, value.

Value came into the world with the first living being, around 4 billion years ago. This pre-dates the arrival of humanity by over 3.9 billion years.

Objective Value

Are values such as good, bad, right, wrong, beauty, ugliness, real in the way that muffins, mushrooms and mountains are? Are values a part of the fabric of the world or are they projections of our own valuing processes? Do we discover values or do we invent them?

Darwin would appear to have assumed that values are part of the fabric of life, and so part of the fabric of the world. Values have been a part of the living world from the beginning. It is fashionable these days to assert that there are no objective values. Values are not real, not part of the fabric of the world. We invent values rather than discover them.

The Australian-born philosopher John Mackie was a prominent exponent of this view. Mackie argues "There are no objective values." [106] "values are not part of the fabric of the world." [107] Mackie seeks to clarify this view. He suggests that:

- The view that there are no objective values is about the status of values rather than any practical, normative view. [108]
- The view that there are no objective values is an ontological claim (about what exists), not a linguistic one (about the meaning of terms). The denial that there are objective values does not commit one to any particular view about what value statements mean. [109] Value judgments include a claim to objectivity, an assumption that there are objective values. This assumption has been incorporated in the meanings of value statements. But this assumption is mistaken. [110]
- The thesis that there are no objective values can be stated that "value statements cannot be true or false." [111] More accurately, value statements may be true or false, but only relative to subjectively agreed and assumed standards – such as in judging dogs at a show or student essays.[112] There is no objective validity about the choice of standards. [113]
- There is a factual difference between kind and cruel actions, but it is not a hard fact that actions which are cruel are to be condemned. [114]

Good health as an objective value

I would claim that there are objective values such as good health. Statements such as "My health is good" may be either true or false – and not just relative to subjectively agreed and assumed standards. States of health – good and bad – preceded subjectively agreed and assumed medical standards by about 4 billion years. Mackie claims

"Something may be called good simply in so far as it satisfies or is such as to satisfy a certain desire." The health of the weeds in my garden may fairly be described as good – they are flourishing - but not insofar as this satisfies (or is such as to satisfy) a certain desire on my part or on the part of the weeds.

Mackie advances several arguments in support of the claim that there are no objective values. The *argument from relativity* begins from variation in moral codes. Radical differences between moral judgments make it difficult to treat these judgments as perceptions of objective truth. Disagreement on questions in sciences such as biology does not show that there are no objective issues in science. But scientific disagreement arises from speculative inferences or explanatory hypotheses based on inadequate evidence. Disagreement about moral codes seems to reflect people's adherence to and participation in different ways of life, rather than perceptions of objective truths. [115]

The argument from relativity does not refute the claim that good health is an objective value. Judgments about the health status of an individual, human or otherwise, may vary, but generally not radically. We mostly agree on the indicators of good and bad health. Most gardeners or farmers can tell a healthy plant from an unhealthy one. You don't need to be a doctor to know the signs of good or ill human health. There are more subtle indicators of good or bad health that require a trained eye to detect. Reading an x-ray photograph for indicators of good or bad health requires extensive training. But these indicators are an objective matter.

It must be admitted that views about the *conditions* for good human health vary more radically. Contemporary Western medicine, Galenic medicine, Chinese medicine and Ayurvedic medicine reflect radically different views about the *conditions* for human good health. It is not easy to tell whether these disagreements reflect scientific disagreement, cultural differences between the societies from which the different traditions arose, or some combination of the two. In the case of non-human living systems, views about the conditions for good health vary less radically. Perhaps this greater convergence of views reflects less curiosity about the conditions for the health of species other than our own, or the greater complexity of humans and of human health.

There does not appear to be sufficient divergence in judgments about indicators of good and bad health to sustain an argument from relativity that good health is not an objective value.

A second argument against the objectivity of values is the *argument from queerness*. Mackie argues that if there were objective values, then they would be entities or properties of a very strange sort. [116] They would have to possess the paradoxical property of being objectively prescriptive – combining objective existence with a power to motivate us to act in certain kinds of ways. An objective good would be sought by anyone who was acquainted with it because the end is objectively prescriptive. [117] Furthermore, if we were aware of objective values, it would have to be by some special faculty, utterly different from our ordinary ways of knowing anything else. [118]

There is nothing, however, very queer about good health, or bad health. It is something most humans would have had some experience of in their own lives. Most people would have perceived it in others. No special faculty is required to perceive good or bad health. Poor health is frequently, though not always, manifest in perceptible symptoms: a sore throat, a runny nose, a headache, or a persistent cough. Our perceptions of our state of health can sometimes be misleading, as in hypochondria. But our "ordinary" perceptions or ways of knowing can also be misleading, as in optical illusions.

Is good health objectively prescriptive? Does acquaintance with it motivate us to seek it? There is a sense in which we are all motivated to seek good health. All living systems work to maintain good health. Good health is an end of all living systems. It is a contingent fact about all living systems that they are so constituted to work to maintain their good health. Furthermore, good health is a basic or fundamental good. [119] For humans, this means resources such as clean air, clean water, good (that is, healthy) food, enough sleep are valued to the extent that they are necessary for good health. Toxins in the air, water or food are negatively valued to they extent that they are harmful to health. So while statements about the state of health of an individual (eg "My health is good") are descriptive, factual statements, they are at the same time evaluative. Acquaintance with facts such as that smoking is bad for one's health *may* in some cases motivate us to give up smoking or never take it up. Value statements are not necessarily action guiding, but they may be.

Mark Platts [120] puts the case against objective values with admirable clarity. He claims that the realist - someone who believes that there are objective values - treats statements of value as descriptions of the world that generally make no reference to human wants or desires.

Such a view appears incompatible with two doctrines, one a dogma of moral philosophy, the other a dogma of philosophical psychology.

The moral thesis is that value statements often serve as reasons for doing (or not doing) some action, together with the claim that, when a person has performed some intentional action, her acceptance of some value statement is her motivating reason for doing it.

The dogma from philosophical psychology is that any complete specification of a reason for an action must make reference to the person's desires or possible desires. [121]

Platts is right to say that the realist treats statements of value as descriptions of the world that generally make no reference to human wants or desires. Statements about the state of health of individuals, human or other, are descriptions of states of these individuals and need make no reference to desires or possible desires. For example the statement "My health is good" is a description of the state of my health but makes no obvious reference to my wants or desires, either actual or possible. The statement "My frangipanni tree is in poor health" is a description of the state of health of a frangipanni tree but again makes no obvious reference to my wants or desires, or those of the frangipanni – presumably it has no wants or desires.

The moral thesis that value statements often serve as reasons for doing (or not doing) some action is also correct. For example, I might stop smoking, or never take it up, because I believe that smoking is bad for my health. In giving up smoking, my acceptance of a value statement "Smoking is bad for my health" may be my motivating reason for giving up smoking.

It does not follow that all or even most value statements are always action guiding. For example, it does not follow that statements such as "My health is good" or "The health of my frangipanni is poor" are action guiding. Adherence to value statements *may* guide action, but it need not. Value statements might be made to inform but not persuade.

Value statements like "I am well" or "My health is excellent" do not serve as reasons for doing, or not doing, anything. The question "How are you?" is a question about your state of health. The reply "I am in excellent health" informs the questioner of your state of health. Neither the question, nor the reply, entails anything about what you should or should not do. Judgments about the good/bad state of health of living systems may or may not be used as a reason for action.

It might be questioned whether statements such as "My health is good" are value statements after all, but, if true, just a plain old fact. The statement "My health is good" is a factual statement but it is also, however, a value statement. It contains a value term "good" and is used to evaluate the state of my health.

I conclude that there are objective values – such as good health.

So what is the difference between a subjective and an objective value? We have seen at the end of Chapter One that a distinction can be drawn between purposes and desires. Recall that purposes but not desires are:

- *universal* to all living systems.
- *intrinsic* to living systems - built into their bodies.
- *objective* features of living systems – their existence does not depend on a conscious subject.
- *innate*, they are inherited genetically.
- *limited* - to survival, reproduction and good health.

Objective values – such as good health – are generated by or are reflections of purposes. Subjective values are generated by or are reflections of wants and desires.

Intrinsic Value

The term "intrinsic value" is highly ambiguous. It is used in different ways by different thinkers, and sometimes in different ways by the same thinker. The different senses of the term "intrinsic value" are somewhat inter-related and can be easily conflated. The multiple meanings of the term have prompted some thinkers to abandon the term and look for other less ambiguous terms to use in its place. But if we are very careful in specifying how we are using the term "intrinsic value" it can be quite a useful term.

All living systems have intrinsic value. I will use the term "intrinsic value" to mean value generated from within the system itself rather than value conferred on it by another system. We sometimes hear it said that all humans are equal. One reading of this is claim is that all humans are of equal worth or value. There is a sense in which not all humans are equal. Some people are valued more than others. Some enjoy higher status and esteem than others. Sometimes this differential status is associated with occupation and position in an organisational hierarchy. In some cases, such as in the caste system in India, differential status accrues to lineage.

Differences in status notwithstanding, some thinkers assert that all people are equal. What could they possibly mean by this? Are these thinkers simply not paying attention? One thing they could mean is that all people are of equal worth or value in the eyes of God. God loves us all equally. God does not discriminate as humans sometimes do. In this sense we are all of equal worth.

There are also secular versions of the claim that all humans are equal. The argument goes that there is some feature of humans – shared by all humans and possessed only by humans – that gives us equal value or worth. The value creating characteristic may be a capacity for self-consciousness, thinking, rationality, autonomy, awakening (Buddha Nature), or language. Some thinkers would go so far as to say that by virtue of possession of these characteristics human life is sacred (or inviolable). This kind of thinking underlies notions of universal human rights.

One way of expressing this claim might be to say that all human beings have intrinsic value, by virtue of possessing some treasured characteristic. Intrinsic value contrasts with value that is conferred on human beings by others, in virtue of occupying a particular position in an organisational or broader social hierarchy.

I will argue that all living systems have intrinsic value by virtue of sharing a common purpose – to live, live well and live better. Intrinsic value in this sense contrasts with conferred value; value that is conferred on a living system by others, perhaps by virtue of that living system's usefulness to other living systems.

John O'Neill distinguishes three different senses of "intrinsic value".

Intrinsic value 1 is a synonym of "non-instrumental" value. An object has instrumental value insofar as it is a means to some other end. An object has intrinsic value if it is an end in itself. Intrinsic goods are goods that other goods are good for the sake of. I have argued good health is an intrinsic good in this sense. O'Neill cites Arne Naess who uses the term "intrinsic value" in this sense in the following passage "The well-being of non-human life on Earth has value in itself. This value is independent of any instrumental usefulness for limited human purposes." [122]

Intrinsic value 2 is a synonym of "non-relational" value. It is the value an object has in virtue of its 'intrinsic properties' O'Neill cites British Philosopher GE Moore who writes, "To say that a kind of value is 'intrinsic' means that the question of whether the thing possesses it, and in what degree it possesses it, depends solely on the intrinsic nature of the thing ...". Intrinsic properties are non-relational. [123]

Intrinsic value 3 is a synonym of 'objective value' – value that an object possesses independently of the valuations of others. Sub-senses depend on how 'independently' is interpreted. It is to deny the subjectivist view that the source of all value lies in valuers – in their attitudes, preferences and so on. [124]

I would suggest a small amendment to O'Neill's intrinsic value 3. Instead of saying that it is a synonym of 'objective value' I would suggest saying it is a synonym of "non-conferred value". I have argued that good health is an objective value in that it is part of the fabric of life and so part of the fabric of the world but it is arguably conferred value in that it is a reflection of the purposes of living systems. I have distinguished objective value from subjective value in terms of the source of the value: whether it arises from purposes (objective value) or desires (subjective value).

Perhaps we could add a fourth sense of intrinsic value:

Intrinsic value 4 is a synonym of 'objective value' – the value that an object possesses by virtue of having purpose conferred on it. It contrasts with subjective value – the value that an object has by virtue of being wanted or desired.

The followed table summarises these for different senses of value:

Intrinsic value	Definition	Contrasts with
1	Basic or fundamental value. An object has intrinsic value in this sense if it is valued for itself rather than valued for the achievement of a more basic end.	Instrumental value
2	Non-relational value – value arising from the intrinsic properties of an object	Relational value
3	Non-conferred value – value that an object possesses independently of the valuations of others – value that does not depend on, arise from or is generated by the valuations of others	Conferred value
4	Objective value – value that arises from purposing rather than wanting or desiring	Subjective value

These definitions over-lap. For example, good health is a basic value, a non-relational value and an objective value, but it is a conferred value – good health could not exist without a valuer. Water is of instrumental and conferred value to a plant, but also of objective value. Political power may be valued for itself, yet is a relational value, a conferred value and a subjective value.

When I use the term "Intrinsic value" I mean "Non-Conferred value" (Intrinsic Value 3).

Living systems are good for something

We saw in Chapter One that living systems are organised for certain purposes. Their parts perform certain functions and they work together (cooperate) in an integrated way to achieve the purposes of the whole such as survival and reproduction. There are significant differences between mechanical systems and living systems. Mechanical systems derive their complexity and purpose from their human makers. Mechanical systems never have their own ends or purposes. They are designed to serve human purposes. The purposes of mechanical systems, then, are *extrinsic* or external to the system.

Not so living systems. Living systems do not derive their complexity and purpose from their makers. *Living systems have their own ends or purposes*, such as maintaining their own good health. That is, some of the purposes of living systems are *intrinsic* or internal to the system. Admittedly, living systems may have extrinsic purposes (they may be valued, differentially, by other living systems). But all living systems have intrinsic purposes.

The question of whether living systems have intrinsic value is closely related to the question of whether they have intrinsic purpose, for as we have seen there is a conceptual connection between value and purpose. Purpose entails value and vice versa. Something that is good is always good *for* something (achieving a purpose). Something that has a purpose is good for that thing.

The connection between purpose and value is revealed in Richard Dawkins' claim that complicated things (biological objects) are "good for something". [125] To say that a thing – an artifact or a living system - is "good for something" suggests it has a use or a purpose – it is good *for* something. It also suggests it is valuable – it is *good* for something. Compare the expression "good for nothing" that means "worthless".

To say that a living system is good for something is to say that "it should succeed in making a living *of some sort*...working to keep itself alive..." [126] All living systems are good for staving off death, and maintaining good health. They are organised to achieve these ends. If all living systems are good for something they must therefore be valuable. Since the ends of a living system are intrinsic to that system, all living systems are intrinsically valuable.

Valuing and Being Valued

In Chapter One we saw that living systems confer purpose, downwards to their parts and horizontally to the requisites for their good health. At the same time, living systems confer *value* on their parts and their needs. The *Macquarie Dictionary* defines "confer" as "to bestow as a gift, favour, honour". I cannot give you something I do not have. Similarly, a living system cannot confer something that it does not have. To confer purpose it must have purpose. To confer value it must have value. Since all living systems confer purpose they must have purpose. By parity of reason, since all living systems confer value they must have value. Value then arises from being valued and from the capacity to value.

All living systems are able to value. To be able to value (give value), a system must have intrinsic value. For how could something that is valueless confer value on its own parts and on the requisites for its own life? If a system is value-less it will have no value to confer. Just as a source of light must be luminous, and a source of purpose (or function) must be purposeful, a source of value must be valuable. Living systems bring good and bad, right and wrong, beauty and ugliness, into the world. They, so to speak, light up the world through the radiance of their own values.

So what property of a system gives it intrinsic value? I have argued it is the capacity of a system to value. This capacity arises from its organisation to achieve its intrinsic purposes.

Living systems are of equal value

The above line of reasoning suggests that all living systems are of equal (intrinsic) value. (Obviously their extrinsic value to other living systems might vary considerably.) The reason for this is that all living systems are equally alive, equally purposeful, equally organised for a purpose, and equally able to value. They are equally value-able and so equally valuable.

But are some living systems better organised than others to achieve their ends? Are human beings better organised than amoeba to stave off death? By the same token, are Desert Oaks from Central Australia that live up to 2,000 years better organised to stave off death than human beings?

While the organisation of living systems is hugely varied it is arguable that all living systems are equally well organised to achieve their ends within the context of their particular way of making a living – or as Darwin would say – their conditions of life. Human beings are well organised for survival and reproduction in the context of their niche and amoeba are just as well organised to achieve these same purposes within their own niche. Humans may differ greatly from amoeba, but not in the quality of their organisation.

It is likely that the quality of organisation of living systems improves over time, as a result of natural selection, as Darwin notes, rejecting traits that are bad, "preserving and adding up all that are good; silently and insensibly working, whenever and wherever opportunity offers, at the improvement of each organic being in relation to its organic and inorganic conditions of life." [127] So while it is arguable that natural selection often slowly improves the organisation of living systems, it would be harder to argue that humans are better organised to achieve their ends than other species, especially when their different organisation is considered in relation to their organic and inorganic conditions of life. As Darwin observes "to suppose that most of the many now existing low forms have not in the least advanced since the first dawn of life would be extremely rash; for every naturalist who has dissected some of the beings now ranked as very low in the scale, must have been struck with their really wondrous and beautiful organisation." [128]

As we will see in Chapter Four, arguably all extant living species are equally evolved, since all living beings are an outgrowth of a single universal ancestor, around 4 billion years ago.

The notion that all living systems are of equal value is sometimes claimed to lead to moral nonsense. It might be thought, for example, that if all living systems are of equal value then to kill an ant or a weed is on a moral par with killing a human being. It is appropriate for a society to have legal sanctions against killing human beings but surely not against killing ants or thistles. It is appropriate to feel great remorse about killing a human but not about killing an ant or a weed. I examine these issues in Chapter Five.

Lee claims that all living systems (at least organisms) are bearers of intrinsic value in the sense of having goods of their own. He suggests that, additionally, humans have intrinsic value in the sense of being able to recognise that natural beings, other than themselves, can be bearers of intrinsic value (in the sense of having a good of their own). Humans uniquely can set about wittingly either to destroy bearers of intrinsic value (that is, a good of their own), or refrain from destroying them. Other animals do not have the consciousness or reasoning capacity that would allow them to do this. Humans are ethical agents in a way that other animals are not, for the capacity to reason enables them to ponder the issue of whether it is right or permissible for humans to kill individual life forms and/or eliminate species. [129]

These additional linguistic and reasoning capacities do make a difference to the kinds of things that are necessary to our flourishing (see Chapter Four) But why should these additional capacities add intrinsic value or inherent worth to humans? They do not make us any more alive, or value-able than other living systems, nor any better organised to achieve our purposes. [130] The additional capacities make us different from but not superior to other living systems.

Features of intrinsic and extrinsic value

Intrinsic value contrasts with extrinsic or conferred value.

It is a commonplace these days to distinguish between the source and the locus of value. [131] As I have defined "intrinsic value" the source of intrinsic and extrinsic value is the same: the valuing activities and capacities of living systems. But intrinsic and extrinsic value has different loci. The loci of extrinsic value can be living or non-living things. Plants confer extrinsic value on non-living things such as sunlight, water, air and soil nutrients, but they also confer extrinsic value on their living parts such as roots, leaves, stems and flowers. Carnivorous plants confer value on their animal prey. Humans confer extrinsic value on their non-living artifacts such as machines or works of art and living artifacts such as gardens. By contrast, the loci of intrinsic value is all and only living systems.

Another contrast between intrinsic and extrinsic value is variability. Extrinsic value varies radically from object to object. The extrinsic value of an object may vary across time. Consider human artifacts as an example. Van Gough's *Irises* (my favourite painting) first sold for 300 francs in 1889 to Octave Mirbeev. Less than a century later the Australian entrepreneur Alan Bond offered $49 million for the same painting. Bond could not afford the price that he offered and the painting was sold to the Getty Museum. The value conferred on the painting, as reflected in its price, varied radically in 100 years. Just as the same painting may vary in extrinsic value over time, at any one time the extrinsic value of different paintings, at least as reflected in their price, may also vary radically.

Not so intrinsic value. Arguably, the intrinsic value of all living systems is equal because all living systems are equally alive, purposive, valuing and well organised for a purpose. The interests of living organisms vary in accordance with their particular way of making a living. The requisites for maintaining good health may differ. Some organisms need oxygen to live. For others, oxygen is a poison. There are more ways to benefit and harm a sentient being than a non-sentient being. But such variations do not affect the intrinsic value of a system. The key question in terms of intrinsic value of living systems is not "Do they suffer?" but "Are they organised for a purpose?" or "Are they able to value?" A living system has the same level of intrinsic value throughout its life span.

When it dies it has no intrinsic value. Life is, in a sense, intrinsic value/purpose. Death is loss of intrinsic value/purpose.

Extrinsic value aggregates in things. One hundred dollars is exactly one hundred times more valuable than one dollar. The same applies to living systems. One hundred cows are one hundred times more extrinsically valuable than one. Not so intrinsic value. One hundred cows have no more intrinsic value than one. You cannot increase the amount of intrinsic value in the world by increasing the number of living systems. A similar logic applies to sacredness. 100 sacred cows are no more sacred than one. As the population of sacred cows grows, the amount of sacredness in the world does not grow proportionally or at all – though if there were no sacred objects there would be no sacredness either.

The following table summarises the contrast between intrinsic and extrinsic value.

Point of comparison	Intrinsic value	Extrinsic value
Source	Valuing	Being valued
Loci	All and only living systems	Living and non-living things

Variability across things	All living systems are equally valuable	Different things have different value depending on degree to which they are valued
Variability across time	Living systems are equally valuable across the life span	Things may vary in value over time
Aggregation	Value does not aggregate	Value aggregates

Value and ethics

The fact that all living systems have intrinsic value has major implications for how we should live. For the fact that something is intrinsically valuable implies that we *should* not harm that thing. In other words harming it is *prima facie wrong.* In other words still, the fact that something is intrinsically valuable is a *good reason* not to harm it. This is not to say that we should never harm that thing – rather that harming it *calls for justification.* Of course, harming it may be justified in certain circumstances.

For example, the fact that a carrot has intrinsic value implies that we should not harm the carrot. The fact that the carrot has intrinsic value is a good reason not to harm it. Harming the carrot calls for justification. But in some cases, harming it may be justified. It may be necessary to harm the carrot because eating carrots or other similar vegetables are necessary to the maintenance of our own good health. Or perhaps harming the carrot is necessary to the maintenance of the good health of a goat whose milk we need to maintain the good health of our selves and/or those with whom we cooperate in a combination of labour in a society.

Alternatively, harming the carrot may be necessary to maintain the good health of a pet horse or rabbit that we care about. With all of these justifications for harming it we may wonder what hope the carrot has got. But we should not harm the carrot without good justification. We should not individually or collectively consume more than is necessary to maintain our own good health.

Many philosophers may be unimpressed by this argument. They might agree that all living systems are intrinsically valuable in a biological sense but this is not sufficient to draw any conclusions about how we should live. It might be argued that having intrinsic value in the biological sense is not ethically significant. We speak of intrinsic value as having ethical significance only when it is defined in terms of the bearer having a cluster of characteristics – consciousness, reason and language – that are unique to humans.

In reply to this argument I would suggest that all intrinsic value is always ethically significant. To suggest that in some cases the value of a thing, however it is defined, has no implications as to how it should be treated seems absurd. If something is of intrinsic value it ought not to be harmed, irrespective of whether "intrinsic value" is defined biologically or in some other way.

The implications of the intrinsic value of living systems for how we should live are examined in the next chapter.

Chapter Three: Ethics

Purpose

All living systems are organised for a purpose – for example, survival and reproduction. It follows that living systems are "good for something" to borrow Dawkins' phrase, so they are valuable. They may or may not be valued by other living systems but all living systems are valuable in themselves – intrinsically valuable. I have suggested that the intrinsic value of living systems arises from their having an intrinsic purpose. Since all living systems are equally purposeful, equally organised for a purpose, equally able to value – equally value-able, I have suggested they are equally valuable.

The famous German musician, doctor and philosopher, Albert Schweitzer recognised that all living systems are purposeful. He expressed this in slightly different language. Instead of saying that all living systems are organised for a purpose he suggested that all living systems have a *will to live*. In saying that living systems have a will to live, Schweitzer was not suggesting that all living systems were conscious or had a conscious will to live. Schweitzer saw the will to live as being innate, an inbuilt disposition of living systems that may or may not be conscious. Schweitzer also appears to have believed that the will to live of living systems gives them value.

Do No Harm

Recognising the equal value of all living systems, what are the implications for how we should live? It seems absurd to say that whether something is valuable or not is completely irrelevant to the issue of how we should treat it for by definition if something is intrinsically valuable it is worthy of reverence or respect. As Schweitzer notes:

> "True philosophy must start from the most immediate and comprehensive fact of consciousness, which says "I am life which wills to live, in the midst of life which wills to live." This is not an ingenious dogmatic formula. Day by day, hour by hour, I live and move in it." [132]

Recognising the equal value of all living systems how should we live? I believe the answer to that question is that we should do no harm to any living system. Schweitzer suggested a similar answer. He wrote: "It is good to maintain and encourage life; it is bad to destroy or obstruct it." The principle that we should do no harm to any living system is called by Paul Taylor "The rule of Nonmaleficence". [133]

Taylor suggests some other principles or rules including the following:

The rule of non-interference requires us to refrain from restricting the freedom of individual organisms, hindering the normal activity and healthy development of a living system and (presumably harmful) intervention with regard to living systems. [134]

The rule of fidelity requires us to refrain from deception of an animal such as is frequently used in hunting, trapping and fishing. [135]

It is not obvious why these rules or principles cannot be subsumed under the principle "Do no harm" since hindering the normal activity and healthy development of a living system and hunting, trapping and fishing are harmful to living systems. That is what makes them wrong.

Exceptions

In saying that we should do no harm to any living system, I am *not* suggesting that harming a living system is never justified. What I am suggesting is the following:

- harming a living system *calls for justification* – but it may be justified
- the principle "Do no harm" is *not absolute*
- the fact that a system is valuable counts as a good reason not to harm that system [136]
- harming a living system is *prima facie wrong* – but not necessarily wrong *all things considered* [137]

The principle "Do no harm", in other words, has exceptions. These exceptions arise from the fact that, because of the way that we are made, it is literally impossible to live by the principle "Do no harm". For example in order to live we must eat. And to eat we must harm other living systems.

Feeding is one of the main forms of interaction between living organisms or lineages in any ecosystem. Feeding relationships are fundamental to the organisation and function of ecosystems: they are fundamental to its flourishing. [138] The main components of an ecosystem can be classified into three categories.

1. Autotrophic organisms: photosynthetic or chemosynthetic organisms with the ability to use light or chemical energy to fix carbon into organic molecules usable as a food source. [139]
2. Heterotrophic organisms: organisms that are unable to manufacture their own food from simple chemical compounds and therefore consume other organisms, living or dead, as their main or sole source of carbon. [140]
3. Detritovores: heterotrophic organisms that feed on dead material (detritus).

Energy and nutrients within an ecosystem flow from autotrophs to heterotrophs to detritovores and back to autotrophs.

Heterotrophs can be grouped into four main categories:

Predators – kill their prey soon after attacking them and consume many different individuals over their lifetime. They may consume part of or all of their prey.

Grazers – attack large numbers of prey (plant or animal) but they may remove only part of each prey individual. Their impact is usually harmful but not lethal in the short term.

Parasites – live in or on their prey, but consume only part of their prey. Their attacks are harmful but rarely lethal in the short term – for this would not be in the parasite's interests. Their attacks focus on only one or a few individuals in a lifetime.

Parasitoids – specialist groups of insects that lay their eggs in or near other insect hosts that the parasitoids eat during their larval stage. [141]

Another way of classifying heterotrophs is in terms of their energy source, as the following table [142] indicates:

Trophic Level	**Energy source**
Herbivores (e.g. cattle, elephants, rabbits, herring, locusts)	Tissues of primary producers (e.g. green plants)
Primary carnivores (e.g. many insectivorous birds, foxes, lions, spiders)	Herbivores
Secondary carnivores (e.g. hawks, seals, sharks)	Primary carnivores
Omnivores (e.g. humans, crabs, many birds)	Organisms from varying trophic levels
Detritovores (e.g. many bacteria, fungi, worms, vultures, fly maggots)	Dead bodies and waste products of other organisms

The flourishing of all heterotrophs, then, and the ecosystems of which they are components, depends on their harming (often fatally) other living systems.

Thus the interests of predators and their prey are in conflict.

This conflict becomes embodied in living systems as a result of the processes of natural selection. Organisms subject to predation have developed defensive mechanisms to avoid harm from predators. These defences include physical defences such as spines or hard protective coatings; chemical defences such as poisons; morphological defences such as blending with their surroundings or behavioural mechanisms such as avoidance or escape activities. [143]

Many animals have immune systems to protect them from microscopic predators such as bacteria or viruses. The immune system is organised to kill would-be predators.

Schweitzer recognised this fact. As Schweitzer put it "The world is a ghastly drama of will-to-live divided against itself. One existence makes its way at the cost of another; one destroys the other." [144] And humans, as heterotrophs, are a part of this drama.

Humans, being omnivores, must harm living organisms to eat. Whether they intend to or not, humans must kill numerous micro-organisms in preventing harmful disease.

We cannot avoid harming living systems by becoming vegetarians since plants are living systems as much as animals. Nor could we avoid harming living systems by becoming fruitarians, eating only fruits, nuts and seeds. Not only would such a diet likely be inadequate for humans, but plants are modular life forms. They are made up many repeatable units, each equivalent to individuals. Each module has its own life cycle, largely independent of the whole. Leaves have a distinct life cycle to flowers. [145] Fruits have a distinct life cycle to roots. Thus in eating fruit or leaves or roots of a plant, we kill an individual. Whatever we eat we kill numerous cells.

We cannot "do no harm" by becoming a vegetarian, a vegan or a fruitarian.

Thus, while harming living systems is always wrong – it calls for justification – harming living systems is in some cases justified. In other words, the ethical principle "Do no harm" has exceptions.

Schweitzer recognised this too. He wrote "Whenever I injure life of any sort, I must be quite clear whether it is necessary." [146]

The principle "Do no harm" can be reformulated as follows:

"Do no harm except as is necessary."

In a letter from Africa, Schweitzer confesses:

> "I have just killed a mosquito that was buzzing around me in the lamplight. In Europe, I wouldn't kill it even if it were bothering me, but here, where mosquitoes spread the dangerous form of malaria,

> I take the liberty of killing them, although I don't like doing it. The important thing is for all of us properly to mull over the question of when damaging and killing are permissible ... Much will be achieved once people become reflective and wisely realise they should damage and kill only when necessary. That is the essence." [147]

So I may do harm when it is necessary to my flourishing. To say that harming a living system is necessary to my flourishing is to say that

1. it contributes to my flourishing and
2. there is no less harmful alternative.

Killing mosquitoes is arguably permissible in Africa, though not in Europe, because it is necessary to curb the spread of malaria. Killing a mosquito may be necessary to my flourishing in Africa because it contributes to the prevention of malaria and there is no obvious way of curbing infection than by killing mosquitoes. Killing a mosquito is not permissible in Europe because, while bothersome, they are not harmful to my health.

Schweitzer claims of a truly ethical person that "If in summer [he] is working by lamplight, he prefers to keep his windows shut and breathe a stuffy atmosphere rather than see one insect after another fall with singed wings upon his table." [148] Let us assume that my working by lamplight contributes to my flourishing. The pursuit of my flourishing, reading by lamplight with the window open, involves killing insects. Killing the insects is not justified in this case because, while reading by lamplight with the window open contributes to my flourishing, there is a less harmful alternative available – that is, closing the window.

Schweitzer believed that harming living systems is permissible even though my harming the system is not necessary directly to my own flourishing. He writes: "The farmer who has mown down a thousand flowers in his meadow as fodder for his cows must be careful on his way home not to strike off in wanton pastime the head of a single flower by the roadside." [149] The harm of mowing down a thousand flowers is justified presumably by its contribution to the flourishing of his cows. The striking off of a single flower "in wanton pastime" is not justified for one "thereby commits a wrong against life without being under the pressure of necessity." [150]

In this case mowing down a thousand flowers is justified not by its contribution to the farmer's flourishing but by its contribution to his cows. The farmer's flourishing may be dependent on the flourishing of his cows, so mowing down a thousand flowers indirectly contributes to his own flourishing. But Schweitzer suggests that my harming a living system may be permissible even in cases where it is necessary to the flourishing of a living system on whom I do not depend for my livelihood. Schweitzer gives the example of four injured pelicans that need to be fed fish in order to live. He writes "I always pity the poor fish to the depths of my soul, but I have to choose between killing the fish or the four pelicans who would surely starve to death." [151]

Feeding the fish to the pelicans is justified, according to Schweitzer, because killing the fish is necessary for the pelicans' flourishing. In this case, Schweitzer considered that killing perhaps thousands of fish was permissible because it contributed to the flourishing of four pelicans. Schweitzer's own livelihood did not depend on the flourishing of the four injured pelicans. But Schweitzer cared for his pelicans.

These cases suggest the following exceptions to the principle that we should do no harm to any living system.

You should do no harm to any living system except as it is necessary to the flourishing of:

1. your self;
2. a living system on which your own flourishing depends;
3. a living system you care about;
4. members of a society to which you belong.

Collectively, as a society, we should do no harm except as it is necessary to the flourishing of:

1. society and its members;
2. living systems on which our flourishing depends;
3. living systems we care about.

A Hierarchy of value?

Do these exceptions imply a hierarchy of value? Is Schweitzer assuming that bacteria are less valuable than humans, flowering plants less valuable than cows, or fish less valuable than pelicans? Many commentators on Schweitzer's ethic have thought so. For example Peter Singer rightly notes that for Schweitzer, life itself is sacred, not even consciousness being necessary for reverence. He also notes correctly that given the breadth of its coverage, it is impossible for the ethics of reverence for life to be absolute in its prohibitions, and that Schweitzer accepts the taking of one form of life to preserve another form of life. Singer questions Schweitzer's claim that all living systems are equally valuable. He writes "Schweitzer's life as a doctor in Africa makes no sense except on the assumption that the lives of the human beings he was saving are more valuable than the lives of the germs and parasites he was destroying in their bodies, not to mention the plants and animals that those humans would kill and eat after Schweitzer had cured them." [152]

Schweitzer's life as a doctor in Africa may make sense on the assumption that humans, indeed all living systems, have a right to self defence against predators. It is not their lesser worth that makes it permissible for Schweitzer to kill bacteria with antibiotic drugs but rather the fact that some bacteria are harmful to human health. Humans would have an equal right to defend themselves against the highly advanced Martian invaders of H G Wells' *War of the Worlds* as they have against the more humble bacteria. In either case we should do no more harm to the would-be predators than is necessary to defend human life and health.

Lawrence Johnson also takes Schweitzer to task over his claim that all living systems have equal value. He notes correctly that the reverence-for-life ethic cannot provide adequate grounds for refusing ever to kill, adding that if we do not kill we cannot live. He notes correctly that Schweitzer did allow that some killing is permissible on the part of a conscientious moral agent. "However, we are immediately confronted with the usual series of problems about where one draws the line." [153] Possibly one way of drawing the line, without resorting to the assumption of differential value of living systems, is to insist on certain exceptions to the principle of doing no harm of the kind outlined above.

Above all, do no harm

I have argued that, recognising the enormous value of all living systems, we should do no harm to them except as necessary for our own flourishing or the flourishing of living systems we depend on or care about. As I will argue in Chapter Four, human flourishing does not consist in getting what we want but in good health, both physical and mental. Aware of the value of living systems we should cultivate compassion and loving kindness to all living systems. We should learn ways to work for the well-being of all living systems – but not by any means.

From the principle "Do no harm" it follows that in the pursuit of our ends – even the most beautiful and noble ends – we should do no harm. That is, we should never use an evil means to achieve any end no matter how worthy. (The only exceptions to this principle are those we have considered above). Thus in seeking to maximise the greater good, minimise harm, and make the world a better place, we should use only non-harmful means.

An end – no matter how worthy – does not justify a harmful means – or only in limited cases. The belief that the goodness of an end justifies an evil means has caused great strife in human history. Our recent history is replete with cases of immense harm being done by a willingness to use harmful means to achieve beautiful ends, such as to save lives, to protect territorial integrity, to protect political sovereignty, to end nasty and, even worse, disobedient regimes, to achieve peace, to spread democracy, to promote law and order, to avenge evil and to resolve conflict. If you have God or Right on your side, all is permitted.

It is perfectly permissible – indeed worthy – for humans to seek to maximise the good and minimise harm, to pursue the welfare of humans and of all living systems. But in doing so we should not use evil means. We should do no harm.

The principle "Above all, do no harm" serves as a check on various maximising and minimising principles such as that we should act in such a way as to maximise flourishing or happiness or minimise harm or suffering. We *should* so act, but only within the constraints that we do no harm to living systems. For example, we may minimise harm or maximise flourishing by the elimination of all carnivores. For a carnivore to flourish over its lifetime, thousands of animals must languish. This is an example of what Schweitzer referred to as the "ghastly drama" of life. On the principle "Above all, do no harm" we should not eliminate all carnivores, because this could only be achieved by doing harm to individual carnivores or at least carnivorous species. It would also harm virtually all ecosystems.

Letting predators be predators

But why should we not eliminate carnivores, if we had the means to do so, to protect the lives of would-be prey? The answer is that living systems have a right to flourish. As human beings we have a right to flourish. The right to flourish includes the following rights:

- a right not to be harmed in life, health and liberty
- a right to do whatever is necessary for us to flourish
- a right to make a living
- a right to harm other living systems to the extent necessary for us to flourish
- a right to kill to eat
- a right to defend ourselves against would-be predators – even if doing so involves killing them.

We have this right not because we are ethical agents and have a choice about how we should live but rather because of the way we are made. We are made to flourish, that is, to stave off death and to maintain good health. As heterotrophs, we must make a living by eating the tissues of other living things. We are made to defend ourselves against predators. For example, a healthy immune system kills predator micro-organisms without us being aware that that is what we are doing.

So, *as a living system* we have a right to flourish. All living systems have a right to flourish.

The right to flourish or make a living is similar to a human right to liberty. The right to liberty is not a right to get what we want. It is not a right to the satisfaction of our interests but rather *the opportunity to pursue our interests*. Our right to liberty is the right to take effective steps to realise the goals we have set for ourselves - to pursue our good as we see fit. But we are not entitled as a matter of moral right to have our good realised. Similarly the right to flourish is the right to pursue whatever is necessary to our flourishing, but not a right to have these interests fulfilled. [154]

To have a right is to have a claim or entitlement to something, binding on an ethical agent. [155] The right to flourish is not generally a claim that the bearer can make on its own behalf. Rather, the value of a living system makes a claim on an ethical agent. The value of a living system counts as a very good reason for an ethical agent not to harm it – except under pressure of necessity.

To eliminate carnivores to protect would-be prey is to violate the carnivores' right to flourish. Carnivores have just as much a right to exist and flourish as herbivores or autotrophs. To eliminate all carnivores would, on a major scale, be to harm living systems without being under pressure of necessity, but in pursuit of a beautiful goal – the minimisation of harm.

What dispositions should we cultivate?

Given the fact that we are highly valuable living systems in the midst of highly valuable living systems what dispositions should we cultivate? In spite of the exceptions to the principle that we should do no harm to any living system, we should cultivate the general disposition to do no harm to any living system – including, of course, our selves.

Schweitzer claims

> Someone is truly ethical only when he or she obeys the compulsion to help all life which he is able to assist and shrinks from injuring anything that lives. Such a person does not ask how far this or that life deserves one's sympathy as being valuable, nor, beyond that whether and to what degree it is capable of feeling. Life as such is sacred to him. Such a person tears no leaf from a tree, plucks no flower, and takes care to crush no insect... If this person walks on the road after a shower and sees an earthworm which is strayed onto it, he bethinks himself that it must get dried up in the sun if it does not return soon enough to ground into which it can burrow, so he lifts it from the deadly stone surface and puts it on the grass. If he comes across an insect which has fallen into a puddle, he stops a moment in order to hold out a leaf or a stalk on which it can save itself. [156]

So for Schweitzer, not only should we dispose ourselves to do no harm but we should cultivate compassion and loving-kindness – at least to the extent of instigating low cost rescue operations for at-risk invertebrates. The Vietnamese Buddhist monk Thich Nhat Hanh also calls on us, in recognition of the value of living systems, to cultivate compassion and loving kindness for all living systems. In his formulation of the first two of the five Buddhist precepts, he writes:

First precept

>Aware of the suffering caused by the destruction of life, I vow to cultivate compassion and learn ways to protect the lives of people, animals, and plants ... [157]

Second precept

>Aware of the suffering caused by exploitation, social injustice, stealing and oppression, I vow to cultivate loving kindness and learn ways to work for the well-being of people, animals and plants ... [158]

Thich Nhat Hanh also calls on us to cultivate compassion and loving-kindness towards our selves.

Fifth precept

>Aware of the suffering caused by unmindful consumption, I vow to cultivate good health, both physical and mental, for myself, my family, and my society, by practicing mindful eating, drinking and consuming ... [159]

Thich Nhat Hanh takes a broad view of suffering as ill-being. [160] Recognising the ill-being caused by harming living systems and implicitly the value of all living systems including ourselves, we should cultivate compassion, loving kindness and good health, both physical and mental in ourselves and in our society.

Philosopher, Paul Taylor discusses those dispositions that enable one to deliberate and act consistently to do no harm. These dispositions accumulate as we mature as character traits that comprise various virtues. He distinguishes two general virtues: moral concern and moral strength. Moral concern is a set of dispositions to "take the standpoint of animals and plants and look at the world from the perspective of their good." Moral concern has four basic constituents: benevolence; compassion; sympathy and caring. [161]

For Taylor living ethically requires more than the cultivation of moral concern. It also requires the cultivation of moral strength. Moral strength includes conscientiousness, integrity, patience, courage, temperance or self-control, disinterestedness, perseverance and steadfastness in duty. [162]

I take a slightly different approach to Taylor. If we cultivate compassion and loving-kindness towards all living systems, including ourselves, then living ethically does not typically require great strength. I would suggest that it requires more self knowledge, and in particular, the capacity to distinguish our needs – the requisites for our flourishing - from those desires and wants the satisfaction of which are not necessary to our flourishing. What is a need and what is a luxury?

We also require a capacity for creativity, imagination and eagerness to learn about practical ways to protect the lives and work for the well being of all living systems. Mindful consumption is an important aspect of this, because, for example, we must kill to eat. Energy consumption indirectly harms living systems – for example, through global warming. As a society, we need to put as much money, effort, organisation and thought into preventing war through peaceful means as we do to preparing for it and fighting it.

Embodied Ethics

Observance of these principles is deeply embedded in most living systems. It is a natural ethic, a natural law – or value system. For example, most living systems will do no harm to most other living systems. Even the most veracious predators will harm living systems only to the extent necessary for them to flourish. In other words, they take what they need but not more than what they need. Most living systems do not over-consume. Predators such as crocodiles, lions and sharks feed relatively infrequently.

Obesity is seldom observed in the animal kingdom. It seems to be confined to human beings, particularly in western countries, and to domesticated animals, such as cats or dogs. Eric Widmaier in his aptly titled book *Why Geese Don't Get Obese (And We Do)* notes that plenty of examples exist in nature of animals that fatten up from time to time. The difference between humans and other species is that the other species fatten up for a reason, such as preparation for hibernation (bears) or migration (geese), whereas humans put on weight for no good reason. [163]

Most non-domesticated species appear to have a functional mechanism to stop them from over eating. This mechanism ensures that they will feel hungry when they need food, but sated when they do not. Widmaier notes that there are well defined centres in the brains of mammals that play a big part in regulating eating behaviour. He notes that the hypothalamus, a tiny part of the brain, appears crucial in regulating eating. [164]

There is strong selective pressure for living systems to follow the principle "Do no harm except to the extent necessary for your own flourishing". Predation is an energy consuming process – it requires hard work. Animals that hunt food only to the extent that they need to are more likely to survive and produce offspring than those that hunt more frequently than necessary. Hunting may be a risky activity and doing so beyond what is necessary would expose an animal to greater risk. Over-eating may also result in obesity and ill-health.

Aggression for its own sake would be harmful to the aggressor, exposing the aggressor to unnecessary risk and an over-expenditure of energy.

If a predator became too effective in killing its prey, and the prey species were not able to find an effective defence, the predator may wipe out the prey species and in the process wipe itself out too. Although a predator may be considered the enemy of its prey, the prey species is certainly no enemy to the predator. Predators are dependent on their prey for their flourishing – indeed survival. Prey species are generally not dependent on predators for their flourishing. (Sometimes they are. Humans are predators of sheep and cattle. These species may not have existed in the numbers they do today if humans did not eat them).

Similarly, members of prey-species tend not to harm their predators any more than is necessary to protect themselves. It may take more energy and exposure to risk to kill, harm, or even fight a would-be predator than to evade it. (He who fights and runs away may live to fight another day. He who just runs away may live even longer).

There are strong selective pressures on animals evading predators rather than fighting them or harming them.

Accordingly animals have embodied the principle of doing no harm. They are likely to harm other living systems only to the extent necessary to their own flourishing and the flourishing of their offspring. They are not likely to defend themselves using any more force than is necessary to protect their flourishing and that of their offspring.

There are selective pressures on parasites to do harm to their host only to the extent necessary for their own flourishing. For a parasite that kills its host risks killing itself. For example, the less harmful a virus is to its host, the more likely the virus is to survive and to replicate. Thus there is a tendency for new strains of viruses to be decreasingly harmful to their hosts. As Steve Jones notes, some viruses have co-evolved with their hosts in such a way that they do no harm to their host at all. They become integrated into the chromosomes of their hosts and are copied each time the host's cells divide. Jones observes "Because such hangers-on *do no harm,* they are transmitted for millions of generations, dormant in the same place in the DNA. Much of our own inherited material is made of such decayed retroviruses, some shared with other primates, others with more distant beasts. Their arrival may have been marked by an epidemic rather like AIDS. If it was, *all hint of bad blood between vehicle and passenger has long disappeared.*" [165]

All living systems, then, appear to have the principle of doing no harm (except insofar as doing harm is necessary for their own flourishing) embodied in them. Human beings it appears are a rare exception to this. Human beings tend to cause harm to other living systems in excess of what they need to flourish. As predators we kill far more than we need for our own flourishing. We sometimes kill just for pleasure rather than need – taking pleasure in the process – e.g. fox hunting – or in the product – e.g. slaughtering baby fur seals for coats. Human beings, particularly in prosperous western societies, tend to over-consume. This is reflected in high obesity rates in these societies.

The law of nature, "Do no harm except as necessary to your own flourishing", appears to be written in the bodies of all species and organisms – except for humans. Humans, to use Australian scientist Tim Flannery's term, are "future eaters". [166] They live beyond their sustainable means. It was not always thus.

60,000 years ago humans lived within their means – they did not eat the future. They lived where their ancestors had lived for over a million years in small groups of hunter-gatherers scattered through parts of Asia, Africa and Europe. They were just one fairly unremarkable omnivore amongst a crowd of other large mammals. [167]

Fundamental changes in ecology are very difficult to achieve in complex, coevolved ecosystems. Humans may have slowly become better predators – but then just as gradually the prey species adjusted – so the balance of power was maintained. Middle Stone Age Africans wisely avoided dangerous species since their weapons were not sophisticated enough to hunt large prey. [168] Other carnivores such as lions and tigers would have preyed upon humans, holding human expansion in check. [169]

Yet by 20,000-50,000 years ago humans developed more varied tools in both form and function. Improvements in weapons meant humans were able to capture bigger fiercer prey. [170] The human occupation of Australia 50,000 years ago suggests ocean-going watercraft. The human occupation of northern Russia and Siberia 20,000 years ago suggests tailored clothing, elaborate houses, elaborate fireplaces and stone lamps. [171] About 30,000 years ago humans began showing a greater aesthetic sense. [172] Some rock paintings in France and Spain date back to this period. Jared Diamond calls this period the great leap forward. [173]

Flannery suggests that such a leap forward could not have taken place in a tightly co-evolved ecosystem such as occurs in Africa and much of Asia. [174] He speculates that migration by humans to new ecosystems such as some islands in the Indonesian archipelago or Australia meant that humans colonised lands in which there were no predators and naïve prey species were plentiful. [175] These ideal conditions enabled the human population to expand in these places and live at hundreds of times the density that was possible elsewhere on Earth. Such a large and dense population, more leisure time and an abundance of resources, would have been conducive to a great leap forward. [176]

Such gardens of Eden could not last forever. Animal resources would have been significantly reduced and a large, dense, human population would become dependent on plants to make a living. This may have been an inducement for the development of agriculture. [177] The great leap forward, having been nurtured in the Eden of

Indonesia must have been carried back to the Afro-Eurasian homeland. [178]

Whatever the origins of the great leap forward, an important point arises from consideration of this event for the relationship between ecology and ethics. For an ethical issue to arise about doing no harm (beyond what is necessary to one's own flourishing) requires fairly unusual ecological circumstances, for in most cases co-evolution ensures that organisms have little choice but to do no harm. It only becomes a problem for humans because around 40,000 years ago they broke free of the ecological straight jacket that constrains most other species, as it did their human ancestors, to do no harm.

Eco-Ethics

Since the second half of the Twentieth Century humanity has entered one of the most harmful phases of its history. Never before have humans caused so much harm to living systems on Earth as we have in the last 50 years, though the seeds of this harm were sewn long before.

Innocent living organisms, not just individuals but entire species are being wiped out - Suzuki claims at the rate of 150 per day! [179] Leakey predicts that by the end of the next century up to 50 percent of the Earth's species may disappear. [180] Few dispute this. Estimates of projected species extinction over the next century vary. This is because it is not known how many species there actually are – estimates vary from ten million to a hundred million. Nor is the size of localities that species are restricted to known. [181]

Leakey identifies three ways in which humans endanger species. The first is through direct harm such as hunting. The second is through the introduction of alien species to new ecosystems. The third and by far the most important are the destruction and fragmentation of habitat, especially, but not exclusively, the destruction of tropical rainforests. [182]

Many human activities or industries are harmful to living systems. These include forestry, farming, fishing/hunting, energy production/conversion and war industries. Most of these industries involve direct harm to living systems. Forestry involves direct harm to trees, farming involves direct harm to farmed plants and animals, fishing and hunting involves direct harm to the animals hunted. Energy production/conversion may involve burning wood, and so involve direct harm to trees. Wars, of course, cause harm to humans (both combatants and non-combatants).

These industries also involve indirect harm to living systems. Felling trees often involves harming the animals that live in and depend on those trees. Farming involves land clearing that kills millions of plants and animals. It also involves the use of herbicides, insecticides and even antibiotics. Fishing may harm animals accidentally caught in nets, and may harm animals (such as penguins) that depend on fish for their survival. Energy production/conversion results in pollution that is harmful to living systems. The extinction of a number of species of amphibians is attributable to global warming (an outcome of pollution caused by burning fossil fuels). Wars cause harm to non-human living systems caught in the cross fire. Testing nuclear weapons must have caused countless deaths and has damaged entire tropical island ecosystems.

The extent of the harm to living systems caused by these industries is a function of the following factors:

- Population size (the number of humans),
- Lifestyle (the per capita use of resources)
- Organisation (advances in the organisational efficiency of these industries)
- Technology (advances in technology associated with these industries).[183]

For example, the extent of harm caused by forestry is a function of the size of the human population (potential consumers of timber), the per capita use of timber products, such as wood and paper, advances in organisational systems designed to maximize tree harvests, and advances in technology to maximize tree harvests (compare the yields of the axe, the chain saw and technology facilitating clear felling). Population and lifestyle impact on the demand for timber products. Organisation and technology impact on their supply.

The extent of harm caused by fishing is a function of the size of the human population, the amount of seafood consumed by each person, as well as organisational and technological advances in fishing (compare the yields of fishing lines with those of drift nets). The use of sonar technology makes finding schools of fish easier.

Clearly, not all advances in organisation and technology increase the harmfulness of an industry. For example, the establishment of national parks, conservation reserves, and marine reserves is an organisational advance, in that it requires high levels of cooperation and trust, as well as effort. A marine reserve is not so much a place as a collective decision of a group of fishers to refrain from fishing in a certain place. Fully protected reserves, areas closed to fishing, protect exploited populations, enhancing production of offspring.

In the energy industry, advances in technology (for example, more fuel efficient cars) can reduce energy consumption. [184] This in turn reduces levels of pollutants such as carbon emissions that are harmful to life. Advances in the design of wind turbines, with blades optimized for low speeds, and larger turbine sizes have seen a rapid increase in the adoption of wind energy on a commercial scale in several European countries – notably, Germany, Denmark and Spain. In these countries laws guarantee fixed price for wind-generated electricity. [185] In 2006, Germany supplied over 5% of its electricity from wind despite not being well endowed in terms of wind resources. The increased adoption of wind energy reduces reliance on the harmful burning of fossil fuels. Writing in 2003, the American energy scientist Vaclav Smil notes that "Direct conversions of solar energy harness by far the largest renewable energy resource but their efficiency and capital and operating costs have, so far, kept them from making a commercial breakthrough comparable to the one experienced by wind power since the early 1990s." [186] In Bavaria, a state of Germany, in 2006, 1% of its electricity was supplied by solar panels, and the rate is doubling each year.

So advances in technology and organisation *may* combine with population and lifestyle to increase the harmfulness of an industry. As Patrick Curry suggests:

Impact = population X lifestyle X organisation X technology [187]

But not always. Sometimes advances in organisation and technology may reduce harm.

How would eco-ethics change the world?

Suppose that people were to dispose themselves to do no harm except as necessary to their own flourishing. How might the world be different?

First, the human population of the earth would begin to decline. It would not decline beyond levels necessary to maintain flourishing societies, but families would seldom have more than two children – the number of children necessary for replacement or a slight decline. It might be arguable that having a child is necessary for the flourishing of some humans (but not all). But having any more than two per family is hardly necessary to human flourishing. Yet each child creates an additional mouth to feed.

Second, consumption, in the developed world at any rate, would also decline. Smil estimates that annual per capita energy consumption of 50-70 GJ is the minimum for a society to satisfy the physical needs of its members and provide for widespread opportunities for intellectual development and respect for basic rights of members. [188]

By this standard many countries over-consume energy. For example, in 1999 annual per capita energy consumption in Germany was 175 GJ. In the United States it was 340 GJ. [189]

Third, industrialization of killing or harm would be likely to decline. Examples of industrialization of killing or harm include:

- clear felling
- land clearing
- drift net fishing
- bottom trawling
- intensive farming.

Clear felling involves the destruction and removal of all or most of the trees in an area called a coupe. Many animals are also killed either directly or indirectly in clear felling. During the felling phase seed capsules are collected from the crowns of felled trees. The seeds are extracted from the capsules and the coupe area is then "slash burned". This involves removal of usable timber and the burning of branches, leaves, discarded logs and flattened vegetation. Once the coupe has been burned the seeds are planted. To protect seedlings from predation, animals that have survived the felling are killed – usually poisoned. An alternative to clear felling is selective felling. Selective felling involves felling of single trees in open forests. Regeneration relies on natural seed fall from retained trees and so there is no need for slash burning. Individual trees can be felled and removed without damaging those left standing. Selective felling involves less harm to surrounding trees and other plants, less harm to the animals living in the forest and less harm to forest ecosystems.

Land clearing is the process of removing vegetation from an area so as to increase the size of the crop producing land base of an existing farm or to provide land for a new farm. Land clearing kills millions of birds and animals each year and is identified as one of the key threats to animal species. An alternative to land clearing is to make more efficient use of land that has already been cleared.

Drift nets are made of plastic or nylon and can be up to 60km in length. They are suspended vertically in the water with floats attached to the top and weights fixed to the bottom. Once set, the nets are then allowed to drift with the wind and currents, entangling any living creature that swims into them. *Bottom trawling* involves towing trawl nets along the sea floor. [190] Bottom trawling can be carried out from one vessel or two vessels fishing cooperatively. Both these approaches result in "bycatch" [191]– non-target fish and other marine life being killed such as dolphins, whales, turtles, sea birds as well as non-target fish. An alternative to drift net and bottom trawling is line fishing or use of small nets closer to the surface.

Intensive farming of animals often involves rearing animals in confined, overcrowded, dimly lit indoor conditions, on bare concrete and slatted floors. Animals have little chance to exercise or graze. This increases the risk of illness, which in turn increases the need for antibiotics.[192] Many laying hens are kept in cramped battery cages in vast sheds with little or no natural light. They have so little space they cannot turn around or stretch their wings. The cramped conditions lead to foot injuries and weak bones. [193]

Increasingly, in what Barbara Noske calls the animal industrial complex, [194] animals are treated as instruments for maximising output (human-wanted substances) at the lowest possible cost or as organic instruments in a laboratory. Much animal activity is directed toward cheap and rapid production of human-wanted things. [195]

Animals are increasingly made to produce in conditions ranging from moderate to total confinement. Confinement systems serve to manipulate them toward increased productivity. In pigs, confinement controls their metabolic activity that might interfere with their maximum weight gaining rate. For hens, confinement serves to control their preference for laying their eggs in nests of their own making. This would put up costs in the way of nest material, space and human labour to collect eggs. The animals' natural capacity for movement, play, preening and social interaction is felt to hinder productivity. [196]

Various chemicals are being introduced as additives in animal feeds that already contain high amounts of calories to maximise productivity. Factory and laboratory conditions often lead to reactions of stress, aggression and fear. If causing economic losses, these reactions are met by even more technology, such as chemical additives to their food. [197]

Noske suggests that the relationship between the animal and its own body has become almost grotesque. The body has become like a machine in the hands of management and is actually working against the animal's own interests. Both the body itself and its functions have been appropriated by the factory management. [198]

Alternatives to intensive farming include free range and organic farming. For example, organic, free range chicken farms allow the bird's free access to organic pasture. They are fed on organic food, not given antibiotics and are kept in small flocks. [199]

These examples of industrialized harm share a number of features in common. On the positive side of the ledger these processes are highly productive and cost effective. The processes contribute to the production of bountiful food and timber products. They are far more productive than their alternatives.

On the negative side of the ledger, these processes are highly harmful to living systems. They not only kill millions of individuals but some threaten entire species, and are disruptive to ecosystems. There are doubts about the sustainability of some of these practices – such as drift net fishing and bottom trawling. Farming animals on an industrial scale may require unsustainable levels of grain production to feed them.

Do the benefits justify the harm? There is reason to doubt it. Global meat consumption has increased by 500 per cent since 1950. Industrial fishing matured in the 1980s. [200] Since that time the global catch in two years was equivalent to all the fish caught in the nineteenth century. We consume per capita far more meat (including fish and chicken) than our ancestors of fifty or a hundred years ago. It is not clear that the vastly increased consumption of meat that industrialization of harm has permitted has contributed to our better health. For example, experience shows that a vegetarian diet can be healthy one. I would not claim that we should all become vegetarians. I would argue that we do not need to eat as much meat as we do, and we do not need to eat as much meat as industrialized harm allows. There are healthy alternatives to meat consumption.

Individuals who dispose themselves to do no harm, except as necessary to maintain their own flourishing are likely to protect life by:

- Establishing reserves – such as marine reserves, forest reserves and national parks. These reserves would be established by agreement to do no harm to living systems in these areas. These reserves would include all remaining old growth forests.
- Refraining from land clearing, preferring to re-use land that has already been cleared
- Reducing the amount of paper, such as through the production and "consumption" of on-line books, magazines, newspapers and journals; double sided printing
- Recycling paper as well as consuming recycled paper products
- Adopting organic and free range farming; and preferring to consume products of organic and free range farming
- Seeking alternatives to use of pesticides, fungicides and antibiotics
- Reducing the scale of farming of animals

- Reducing the use of coal and oil and increasing the use of renewables such as solar and wind energy. This could be at a small local scale (such as solar hot water systems) or industrial scale.
- Conserving energy such as through the increased use of public transport, more fuel efficient cars (such as hybrid cars), more energy efficient electrical appliances and more energy efficient light bulbs
- Cultivating peace by
- Conflict resolution forums
- Inter-faith dialogue
- Disarmament
- Non-violent, non-cooperation
- Peace Studies
- Increasing social justice
- Reducing conditions that contribute to war.

The following table shows industries that are likely to flourish and those that are likely to decline in a world in which individuals dispose themselves to do no harm.

Area	Flourishing industries	Declining industries
Forestry	Forestry protection and conservation including reserve management	Intensive forestry
	Selective felling in open forests	Clear felling
	Fine carpentry – adding value	Wood chipping
	Recycling of paper and timber products	
Fishing	Marine protection and conservation including reserve management	Industrial scale fishing
	Line fishing, fishing close to the surface	Drift net fishing and bottom trawling
Farming	Organic and free range farming	Intensive farming, particularly of animals
	Reuse of land that has already been cleared	Land clearing

	Alternatives to use of pesticides, fungicides and antibiotics to preserve the flourishing of farm animals/plants	Pesticides, fungicides, antibiotics
Energy	Solar energy, wind energy	Coal and oil
	Public transport	Private transport
	Increasing energy efficiency of machines and processes	
Military/Peace	Conflict Resolution/ Peace Studies	Military industry – both public and private
	Inter-faith dialogue	
	Non-violent non-cooperation	
	Disarmament	Arms production
	Peace activism	War activism

Education	Cultivating disposition to do no harm	
Training	Cultivating skills to support less harmful industries	
Tourism	Eco-tourism – small scale – local	
Finance Industry	Ethical investment	
Legal Industry	Judicial activism to protect life	

Conclusion

All living systems are of value and of equal value. It follows that you should do no harm to any living system except as it is necessary to the flourishing of:

1. your self;
2. a living system on which your own flourishing depends;
3. a living system you care about;
4. members of a society to which you belong.

To say that harming a living system is necessary to your flourishing is to say that it contributes to your flourishing and there is no less harmful alternative.

From the principle "Do no harm" it follows that in the pursuit of our ends – even the most beautiful and noble ends – we should do no harm. That is, we should never use an evil means to achieve any end no matter how worthy. (The only exceptions to this principle are those considered above). Thus in seeking to maximise the greater good, minimise harm, and make the world a better place, we should use only non-harmful means.

This account raises two questions. First, what is human flourishing? (If human flourishing consists of getting what you want then the principle "Do no harm except as necessary to human flourishing" would be too permissive – it would amount to saying "Do no harm except as necessary to get what you want.") Second, how can we account for the strong moral intuition that it is more seriously wrong to harm a human than a bacteria or an insect if all living systems are equally valuable?

I answer the first question in Chapter Four and the second question in Chapter Five.

Chapter Four: Human Flourishing

All living systems have the capacity to flourish or languish. What does human flourishing consist of? For living things to flourish is to be healthy. [201] For living things to languish is to be unhealthy. In other words the basic good of a living system is good health, where "health" is taken in a very broad sense to include physiological and psychological wellbeing – that is effective overall integrated functioning. [202] German philosopher Hans-Georg Gadamer characterizes good health in terms of equilibrium. He suggests "medical intervention must be understood as an attempt to restore an equilibrium that has been disturbed..." [203] Understanding good health in terms of equilibrium goes back at least 2,500 years to Aristotle and Hippocrates. According to Hippocrates symptoms are not the disease itself but are an attempt by the body to restore its balance. A physician cannot cure – only the body can do that – but a physician can correct the conditions that throw the body out of balance or equilibrium. [204] For human beings in particular, psychological health is an important component of flourishing. [205]

Human Flourishing: Getting What You Want?

What does good psychological health consist of? According to a common account, good psychological health consists either of the experience of pleasure and the absence of pain or it consists of getting what we want. According to such an account, pleasure is intrinsically good and pain is intrinsically bad for one. Satisfaction of desire is intrinsically good and frustration of desire is intrinsically bad. Hedonistic Utilitarianism takes pleasure to be intrinsically good and pain to be intrinsically bad. Preference Utilitarianism takes the satisfaction of desire to be intrinsically good and the frustration of desire to be intrinsically bad. Act Utilitarianism proposes that one should act in such a way as to maximize the good – whether the good is conceived as pleasure or satisfaction of preferences.

From an evolutionary perspective, however, pleasure is not an intrinsic good but an instrumental good. Pain is not an intrinsic evil, but often an instrumental good. It is true that pain feels bad, but that is why it can be instrumentally good.

A consideration of the main ideas of evolutionary psychology can help to see this. Edward Hagan notes that in the past few centuries physiologists have revealed details of the functional organisation of the physical body. Their discoveries suggest that the structure of the body serves survival and reproduction. In addition, most biologists acknowledge that this functional structure is an outcome of natural selection. In the last hundred years, psychologists have developed powerful techniques that suggest that cognition, too, has structure.

Evolutionary psychologists conjecture, plausibly, that cognitive structure, like physiological structure, has been "designed" by natural selection to serve survival and reproduction. Since virtually all tissue in living organisms is functionally organised, and because this organisation is the product of evolution by natural selection, a major presumption of evolutionary psychology is that the brain or the mind, too, is functionally organised, and best understood in an evolutionary perspective. This is the foundational assumption of evolutionary psychology. Evolutionary biologists refer to the functional components of organisms as 'adaptations'. Evolutionary psychologists often refer to brain functions as psychological adaptations, although they are not qualitatively different from other adaptations. [206]

But if psychological structures such as pleasures, pains and desires are adaptations, then they are a means toward an end – survival and reproduction. They are instrumentally good but not intrinsically good or bad. The pleasure-pain mechanism in the bodies of all sentient living organisms serves as a guardian of the organism's life. The physical sensation of pleasure signals that the organism is pursuing the *right* course of action. The physical sensation of pain signals that the organism is pursuing the *wrong* course of action, that something is impairing the proper function of its body, which requires action to correct it. [207] For example, if we put our hands on a hotplate we will feel pain. This signals that we are pursuing the wrong course of action – by harming our hand, and action – removal of the hand from the hotplate – is necessary to correct this wrong course of action.

Pleasure, then, is a *signal* or *indicator* to an organism that the organism's action is conducive to its good health. Pain is a *warning signal* to an organism that something is impairing the proper function of its body, which requires action to correct it. Pain is a *signal* of poor health.

To suppose that pleasure is an intrinsic good is on a par with supposing that a finger pointing at the moon *is* the moon. Like the finger pointing at the moon, pleasure and pain are a signal, or indicator of something (a good or evil) beyond it.

Pain, then, is not an intrinsic evil. In fact, when functioning as it should, it is an instrumental good. Clearly, the pleasure/pain mechanism is good for the health of an organism. The capacity to feel pain is an instrumental good to an organism. A person with congenital insensitivity to pain has a poor prognosis. Overheating kills more than half of all children with this condition before the age of three. Pain is also an instrumental good *provided* the pain can be avoided.

Similarly, from an evolutionary perspective, mental states such as beliefs and desires evolved to orientate their bearers: to guide them to pursue what is beneficial to them and avoid what is harmful to them. In general an organism is motivated to pursue what is good for it and avoid what is bad for it. Not, however, always. Sometimes humans can be motivated to over-consume, or to consume toxins such as nicotine. In this case getting what you want may be bad for you. It is possible for a human to be motivated to under-consume. Anorexia Nervosa is a mental disorder, most common in adolescent girls, causing an aversion to food, which may lead to serious malnutrition. [208] The anorexic is often motivated to avoid food to lose weight. This desire is rooted in the delusional belief that she is overweight. The satisfaction of the anorexic's desire may be harmful and even fatal to her.

The satisfaction of a desire is good for you to the extent that its satisfaction facilitates your good physical or mental health. It may be bad for you if its satisfaction is out of alignment with your physical and mental health. To the extent that the satisfaction of a want is good it is an instrumental good, not an intrinsic one. In some cases the satisfaction of a desire may not be good for you. Pleasure and satisfaction of desire are good or bad for us only in terms of our good health. [209]

Human Flourishing: Good Health

From an evolutionary perspective what is basically good for us is survival. All living systems have an urge to survive programmed into them, as it were, by natural selection. Beings with the strongest urge to live tend to live longer, have more offspring and pass on such characteristics to their offspring. Living systems are not content with mere survival. Natural selection also favours those with a will to live, to live well and live better. [210] So from an evolutionary perspective what is good for us is not getting what we want so much as getting what we need for survival and good health.

An interest in reproduction?

Is reproduction good for us?

Maynard Smith and Szathmary claim that a common feature of a number of transitions from simpler to more complex forms of life is that individuals with a capacity for independent replication before the transition are no longer capable of independent replication after it. This raises a common problem. Why did selection between entities at the lower level not disrupt integration at the higher level? For example, why would an individual ant "sacrifice its chances of reproduction to help the colony"? [211]

They quote ornithologist V C Wynne Edwards who pondered, given the enormous reproductive capacity of most animals, why their numbers do not increase until the food runs out and they starve. Why does the reproduction rate of many living organisms slow when food is scarce? His answer was that such behaviour "although beneficial to the population by preventing starvation, is harmful to the individuals that do not breed. Therefore, he argued, such self sacrificing behaviour requires group selection." [212]

In wondering at the sacrifices made by organisms in giving up reproduction these biologists appear to be overlooking a rather important fact about reproduction – that it is hard work. If we see reproductive work as a chore, then it is no harder to understand why an individual ant should give up reproduction to specialise in some other task, than to "sacrifice" its chance to forage most of its life.

In seeing foregoing reproduction as a sacrifice or as harmful, these writers appear to assume that organisms have an interest in reproduction. But reproduction is not straightforwardly a benefit. For example in trees production of fruits and flowers is expensive. Young trees cannot afford to reproduce and older trees do so at cost. Reproduction slows growth in height and width. Flowers take the place of some leaves. [213]

Possibly, the view that giving up reproduction is a sacrifice reflects a male perspective. Larger costs tend to be involved in maternal reproduction. For example, in most mammalian species the contribution to and cost of reproduction tends to be greater in the female than the male. In trees with distinct male and female individuals, such as poplars, males tend to be taller and live longer because of lower reproductive effort and costs. [214] Reproduction of individuals is of greater benefit to the lineage than it is to the individual.

Are we harmed by not reproducing? Clearly, a child is not harmed by the fact that he/she has not reproduced. So at what age does not having reproduced become harmful? At puberty? Or for females, at menopause? If reproduction is a benefit, does it follow that the more children the better? It is not obvious that an individual is harmed by not reproducing.

It could be argued that reproduction is an integral part of the adaptation problem for all living species, and a considerable part of our collective activity as a species is involved with reproduction. [215] This is true. Few would deny that reproduction of at least some individuals is a benefit to a species or lineage. This does not show it is a benefit to an individual. Also note that the flourishing of our species does not depend on all of us having children.

It might also be argued that reproduction is a very strongly felt desire for a vast number of humans. [216] For many people having children gives them a sense of connection and meaning in life. But a meaningful life is possible without having children. A person can contribute to their society, to humanity, or to the wider living world, without reproducing - for example, St Francis of Assisi, Beatrix Potter, the Dalai Lama, or Jane Austen. Reproducing is but one means towards that end. A sizable minority of humans do not want to reproduce.

In Plato's dialogue The Symposium Diotima argues that "mortal nature seeks, as far as may be, to perpetuate itself and become immortal. The only way it can achieve this is by procreation, which secures the perpetual replacement of an old member of race by a new." [217] Is immortality not a benefit to an individual? I would agree with Diotima that a person's descendents are in a sense their continuation. However, procreation does not turn a mortal into an immortal. Procreation does not change one iota the inevitability of a mortal's eventual death.

Internal Harmony

Good health has physiological and psychological aspects. So what then is intrinsically good for us psychologically? One component, at least, of what is good for us is integrity or internal harmony. Whatever disrupts internal harmony or integrity is bad for our health and bad for us. Whatever contributes to internal harmony or integrity is good for our health and good for us. Internal harmony appears to be basically or intrinsically good for us. Internal conflict or disharmony seems intrinsically bad for us.

In other words, human flourishing consists in part in internal harmony. (I will argue later that another component of human flourishing is a sense of connection). Human languishing consists in part in internal disharmony and conflict.

Taxonomies of mind

Thinkers disagree as to exactly what the parts of our minds are. In his Dialogue *The Republic* Plato suggests that the human psyche consists of reason, appetites (desires) and "spirit" emotions (such as anger or indignation). "We can call the reflective element in the mind the reason, and the element with which it feels hunger and thirst, and the agitations of sex and other desires, the element of irrational appetite – an element closely connected with satisfaction and pleasure" [218]– Plato has Socrates say. Anger, Socrates argues, "is different from desire and sometimes opposes it." [219]

Canadian social commentator John Ralston Saul speculates that the list of our qualities is Common Sense, Ethics, Imagination, Intuition, Memory and Reason. He suggests that each quality takes its meaning from the other – from the tension in which they exist with each other. [220] For both Plato and for Saul – we flourish to the degree to which we achieve internal harmony (Plato) or equilibrium (Saul) between the different elements. Plato suggests that in a just person – a person in balance – reason rules. 'So the reason ought to rule, having the wisdom and foresight to act for the whole, and the spirit ought to obey and support it.' [221]

It is possible to imagine an internal harmony being achieved between the parts of the mind without one dominating the other. Socrates conjectures that a concord between reason and "spirit" can be achieved by intellectual and physical training that "tunes up the reason by a training in rational argument and higher studies, and tones down and soothes the element of "spirit" by harmony and rhythm." [222] Tuning up, soothing and toning down falls short of domination. Socrates concludes that a "just man" – and we could equally say a flourishing or healthy person – "will not allow the three elements which make up his inward self to trespass on each other's functions or interfere with each other, but, by keeping all three in tune, like the notes of a scale (high, middle, and low and any others there be), will in the truest sense set his house to right, attain self-mastery and order, and live on good terms with himself. When he has bound these elements into a disciplined and harmonious whole, and so become fully one instead of many, he will be ready for action of any kind..." [223] The musical metaphor does not imply a relationship of domination of one part of the psyche over another. All the notes are equal – unless a hierarchy is supposed, and it need not be, in the high, middle and low.

We might not agree with Socrates' view of the elements of the self, but still agree that flourishing consists, in part, in internal harmony – the various parts of a person working harmoniously together to survive - that is to live, to live well and to live better.

The disruption of internal harmony

Internal harmony, and flourishing, may be disturbed if our desires are in conflict with our needs. A desire to smoke is an example. The anorexic's desire to lose weight is another example. These desires may also be in conflict with other desires such as a desire to live a long and healthy life, or the desire for physical fitness.

An extra-marital affair (especially a clandestine affair), may be damaging because it puts at risk the love of someone whom you love. [224] Having to hide a forbidden love, perhaps to vehemently deny what you know to be true, to have to pretend that you don't have feelings that you know you do, is deeply disruptive of internal harmony. Clandestine affairs involve living a lie. In extreme cases it may lead a person to live a double life. Since we only have one life, leading a double life is highly disruptive to internal harmony and to flourishing.

Internal harmony (our integrity) may be disrupted if our convictions are out of harmony with our actions. If you are of the conviction that killing sentient life is wrong, but given a choice between eating vegetables and eating meat you tend to choose meat then your convictions are out of harmony with your actions (unless you believe that eating meat is necessary for your own good health). Suppose you are of the conviction that killing sentient life is wrong, but you buy and consume meat from a different butcher each week over the course of a year. This way you may not generate additional demand for meat products and no more animals may be killed as a result of your consuming them than you would have if you did not consume them. Suppose you hide the fact that you are doing this, and you advocate a vegetarian lifestyle. Then while you may avoid generating demand for meat, you may be doing harm to yourself – disrupting your internal harmony by not practicing what you preach.

Making a livelihood in a way that conflicts with your convictions about how you should live disrupts inner harmony and flourishing. For example, if you are a pacifist – perhaps a peace activist – working in the arms industry would disrupt your internal harmony. Even if you could persuade yourself that if you did not do it somebody else would, you would still be doing great harm to yourself by working in that industry. Working for an employer whose policies or practices run counter to your convictions may be harmful to you. In some cases your employer may make decisions you personally disagree with out of consideration for a broader constituency. Suppose that decision were reached democratically – by a process that you support. In these circumstances it may be possible to work for that organisation – and even implement the decision – without harming yourself.

Sometimes we can be harmed by having too much negative emotion. [225] If you find yourself in a situation where you feel angry most of the time, such as might happen if you are working for an employer who you do not get along with, or in an organisation whose policies you feel are unjust, or perhaps in an unhappy marriage, then you do harm to yourself by continuing in that employment or marital relationship. You may feel unable or unwilling to leave it, but while you are in it you do harm to yourself.

I have suggested that good health is an intrinsic good for all living systems including humans. Good health has physiological and psychological aspects. One component, at least, of what is good for us psychologically is integrity or internal harmony.

A Sense of Connection

A second component of what is good for us psychologically is a sense of connection. A sense of alienation or estrangement is intrinsically bad for us, psychologically. All earthly living systems are deeply interconnected with each other. To the extent that we have a deep sense of connection with all living systems we live well – we have good psychological health. To the extent that we have a sense of alienation from living systems we suffer from delusion and our psychological health is less than optimal.

Interconnections in Darwinian Time

We tend to see ourselves as being separate from others. We tend to perceive sharp boundaries between our selves and other humans, between humans and other living systems, between sentient and non-sentient life and between the living and non-living world. One of the most profound insights uncovered by Charles Darwin is that all Earthly living organisms are connected to each other in time. All extant life has a common ancestor.

Darwin believed that all species on Earth are related through a process of descent. Darwin writes "It is a truly wonderful fact – the wonder of which we are apt to overlook from familiarity – that all animals and all plants throughout all time and space should be related to each other in groups, subordinate to groups in the manner which we everywhere behold – namely varieties of the same species most closely related, species of the same genus less closely and unequally related, forming sections and sub-genera..." [226] And similarly for families, orders, classes (and presumably kingdoms).

Darwin uses the simile of the tree to describe the relationships of descent between living beings. He writes:

> The affinities of all the beings of the same class have sometimes been represented by a great tree. I believe this simile largely speaks the truth. The green and budding twigs may represent existing species; and those produced by former years may represent the long succession of extinct species...The limbs divided into great branches, and these into lesser and lesser branches, were themselves once, when the tree was young, budding twigs... Of the many twigs which flourished when the tree was a mere bush, only two or three, now grown into great branches, yet survive and bear the other branches...As buds give rise by growth to fresh buds, and these, if vigorous, branch out...so by generation I believe it has been with the great Tree of Life, which fills with its dead and broken branches the crust of the earth, and covers the surface with its ever-branching and beautiful ramifications. [227]

Humanity – the species *Homo sapiens* – is but a tiny green and budding twig in the great Tree of Life.

It appears that all extant life on Earth has descended from a single ancestor (though not necessarily the first living being. [228] Other living beings may have been generated before the universal ancestor and produced lineages that sooner or later died out.) Evidence of a universal ancestor includes a universal genetic code in all life on Earth. It seems unlikely that such a specific and rather quirky code would have arisen many times independently. Mechanisms for reading that code and producing proteins are highly similar in all living organisms. [229]

The features of the great Tree of Life are better known today than they were in Darwin's day. The trunk of the tree is the Kingdom Monera – single celled bacteria. Mergers between bacteria resulted in the first major branch in the tree of Life – Protoctists (including algae, slime moulds and ciliates). Animals, plants and fungi developed from mergers between Protoctists and various bacteria. [230]

It is humbling to consider what a recent arrival *Homo sapiens* is. If we represent the time since the origin of life (around 4 billion years ago) as a single day the first kingdom (Monera) began at midnight. It was not until 1:51**pm** that the second kingdom (Protoctists) appeared. The third kingdom (Animals) did not appear until 8:25pm. The fourth and fifth kingdoms (Plants and Fungi) turned up around 8:46pm. With the five kingdoms all in place at just after quarter to nine, mammals arrived at 10:14pm. The primates appeared at 11:46pm. It took until 11:58pm (and 34 seconds) for the genus Homo to arrive. Archaic forms of *Homo sapiens* appeared at 5 seconds to midnight, and were fully evolved by 2 seconds to midnight.

Darwin's "truly wonderful fact" is in tension with our notion that we are separate selves. Implications include:

- All life is connected through Darwinian time. [231]
- All extant living beings on Earth are kin, having descended from a single, tiny, universal ancestor.
- Life is a unity. Each of us belongs to a single primal ground. [232]
- Life is a unity and a manifold at the same time. Just as a tree is one being with many branches and twigs, life is a single entity with five main branches (kingdoms), numerous sub-branches (classes), and even more numerous twigs (species - ninety nine percent of which have died out).
- Humanity is no more highly evolved than other species. All extant living species are equally evolved [233] – but adapted to different conditions and to occupy a different niche – a different way of making a living.
- I do not have a separate self. All exist as part of a wonderful stream of life which is constantly moving. [234]
- As Margulis and Sagan observe "From an everyday, uncontentious perspective, "you" began in your mother's womb some nine months before whatever your age is. From a deeper, evolutionary perspective, however, "you" began with life's daring genesis – its succession more than 4,000 million years ago, from the witches' brew of the early Earth." [235]
- Thich Nhat Hanh puts it more poetically. "The disintegration of this body does not touch me, just as when the plum blossom falls it does not mean the end of the plum tree." [236]

- I am one with the wonderful pattern of life that radiates out in all directions. [237]
- I am in my ancestors and they are in me. [238]
- My ancestors are in me because they produced me. The genetic code I carry in every cell of my body, the machinery for reading it and for producing the proteins that constitute my body, I inherited from the universal ancestor or from its early descendants. The redness of my blood I inherit from my sulphate breathing ancestors that synthesised a molecule called a porphyrin ring. This bright red molecule circulates in our blood today, where it is used to carry oxygen to our cells. [239] My capacity to breathe oxygen is inherited from the ancestors of my mitochondria that developed oxygen mediated metabolism. [240] My capacity to bypass oxygen-mediated metabolism and revert to the ancient fermenting mode, when I exert myself, is inherited from my anaerobic ancestors that converted sugars to energy through fermentation. [241]
- I am in my ancestors because my existence is sufficient (though not necessary) for their existence.
- You and I are one in that we share the same primal ground, and a large slice of common ancestry going back 4 billion years. We are "outgrowths" of the one great Tree of Life.

Interconnections in Vernadskian Space

The early Twentieth Century Russian Scientist Vladimir Vernadsky also taught that life is a unity, and that all life

– or living matter – is connected in space. He writes "all life is an indivisible unity with regular connections between its parts, but also the inert matter surrounding the biosphere." [242] The biosphere is the domain of life – effectively the whole surface of the Earth.

Vernadsky understood that from a geological perspective all humanity is one. He writes "The geologic evolutionary process corresponds to biological unity and equality of all people in *Homo sapiens* and his geological ancestors...It is a natural law: All races interbreed and give fruitful progeny." [243]

For Vernadsky, humanity is inseparable from living matter. He argues that from within the pressures of present-day life, we tend to forget that we and the whole of humanity cannot be separated. We are a part of the biosphere and closely connected to all its inhabitants. Vernadsky writes that "Man is commonly referred to as an individual, freely living and moving over our planet and freely building his history....In reality, not a single living organism exists on Earth in a free state. All these organisms are constantly and inseparably connected with their matter-energy surroundings by their nutrition and respiration." [244]

Most of us think of our selves as solid and stable. By contrast, Vernadsky compares life to a torrent or a whirlpool. For example he writes

> Atoms absorbed by some form of life, caught by a singular torrent of life, hardly, if at all, return to the inert matter of the biosphere... The new generations produced by propagation absorb

> atoms from the changing surroundings and retain
> them in the whirlpools of life by carrying them from
> one to another. [245]

In torrents and whirlpools there is an enormous flow-through of elements.

> One of the most important manifestations of life in
> the biosphere is the gas exchange of organisms with
> their gaseous surroundings. Part of this gas
> exchange...is *burning*. In this way atoms of carbon,
> hydrogen and oxygen are constantly leaving and
> entering the whirlwinds of life in great masses. [246]

Living matter is a unity. Vernadsky considered that living matter is transformed sunlight. He suggests that life and living matter may be conceived as an indivisible whole in the mechanism of the biosphere. He notes that only part of it immediately utilises solar rays, namely, the green plants. The whole living world – for example the animal kingdom - is directly and indissolubly connected with this green photosynthesizing part. He writes "Animal matter and that of plants containing no chlorophyll are further developments of the same processing of chemical compounds created by green plants. So all these parts of living nature may be envisaged as the process of further transformation of the luminous solar energy into active energy of the Earth." [247]

We are sunlight. Vernadsky writes "Great ancient religious intuitions of humanity that regarded terrestrial creatures, especially human beings as "children of the Sun" were much nearer the truth than theories considering them to be an ephemeral product of blind and accidental transformation of Earth's matter and forces." [248]

We are air. Vernadsky writes "Living matter can be considered an appendage of the atmosphere." The bodies of plants and indirectly our own bodies are created from the gases of the atmosphere (e.g. carbon dioxide). Life then converts them into combustible matter by involving the cosmic energy of the Sun. [249]

We are water. Vernadsky observes that water on average comprises much more than two-thirds of living matter's mass. In addition, the presence of water is essential for their reproduction, metabolism, and function within ecosystems and the biosphere. Vernadsky goes so far as to say "Not only is water in the biosphere inseparable from life – life is inseparable from water." [250]

We are the Earth. Vernadsky writes "The diffusion of green living matter in the biosphere through propagation is one of the most characteristic and significant manifestations of the Earth's crust." [251]

To summarise, all living beings are connected in Darwinian time and Vernadskian space. Human flourishing in part depends on recognizing this – on having a sense of connection.

Connection and Flourishing

Concepts of connectedness inform traditional and contemporary Australian Aboriginal culture. In a wonderful film entitled *Kanyini* by a young film-maker

Melanie Hogan, Bob Randall, a traditional Aboriginal owner of Uluru in Central Australia, describes the concept of Kanyini – connectedness – and its significance for the Aboriginal people of Central Australia.

In the film Bob Randall describes the prevailing belief system as a boy growing up in an Aboriginal community in Central Australia.

> "Growing up with the oldies our parents, grandparents – they always said we are connected to everything else and the proof of that is being alive. Being alive connects you to every other living thing that's around you. Your spirit, your psyche, your physical, your mental - you are connected with other living forms. You are never lost, you are never alone. You are one with everything else that's there. The Oneness – the completeness of the Oneness!"

Randall's account of connectedness resonates with Darwin's tree of life and Vernadsky's biosphere. Venturing beyond Darwin and Vernadsky's territory, Randall describes in vivid and poetic terms the significance of a sense of connection to human flourishing. He describes the joy that flows from bringing a sense of connection with all living beings into your whole way of life.

> "Living in the bush gives you the confidence of life that you can never be trained into. It's so much a natural part of life. You are communicating with everything – the wind, the trees, the flowers, the grass and every action is an action of beauty and awareness and like "How are you today?" It's that

niceness, that connection that makes you feel so good."

Describing the way of life in Central Australia for Aboriginal people prior to the European occupation, Randall identifies the contribution that living with a sense of connection makes to human flourishing.

> "In our way, in the traditional way, all that is around you that you are walking on, the air you are breathing, the water you are drinking is yours and the confidence is an automatic part of you. You grow big and strong because you are walking with all the other big things and strong things together. There are no weak things in that. That confidence is a reality. You feel it, you think it, you walk it."

Connecting with the land and with life nourishes and expands us. It gives us confidence. That sense of connection is above all good for us. Reflecting on the traditional way of life he experienced as a child growing up in Central Australia, Randall recalls

> "We weren't starving hungry. We weren't covered with sores living out there in the bush. I can picture some of my old people before they wore clothes and they look as well as anyone in the street without their clothes on... In the naturalness and the beauty of the naturalness... they were looking really well. Their spirit looked good, they physically looked good, they were beautiful people because they lived in a beautiful way."

This is a most elegant description of human flourishing flowing from a life lived in a deep sense of connection with living beings and the land. Randall also eloquently describes the languishing flowing from the loss of a sense of connection. He movingly describes the awful effect on the Australian Aboriginal people of the dispossession of their land, the policies of removal of so called "half-caste" Aboriginal children from their parents – the stolen generation – and the imposition of Christianity and European ways of life on Aboriginal people at the hands of the Christian missionaries, supported by Australian Governments.

> "You take away my Kanyini – my connectedness – my life – the essence of all I'm here for, my purpose. You take that away and I am nothing. I'm dead. I'm nothing. I'm a living dead, I'm a corpse in space. And that's what the Government did. I became nothing. It took away that Kanyini. Once forced to live without that – this is when the dependency comes in and you will die. You can almost say the time of death is the moment you accept that... Its suicide."

A deep sense of connection to life and the earth is vital to the flourishing of all human beings. Without it we languish.

French philosopher Luc Ferry would challenge the idea that human flourishing consists in part in a sense of connection. He writes:

> "Our entire democratic culture, our entire economic, industrial, intellectual, and artistic

> history since the French Revolution has been
> marked, for basic philosophical reasons, by the
> glorification of *uprootedness,* or *innovation,* which
> amounts to the same thing – a glorification which
> romanticism, followed by fascism and Nazism,
> have continually denounced as ruinous to national
> identity, even to local particularities and
> customs." [252]

In fact, the currents that inform our democratic culture, our economic, industrial, intellectual and artistic history are far more varied than Ferry suggests. For example, our democratic culture is informed by the notion of citizenship, of the rights and responsibilities associated with our belonging to or rooted to a community. Similarly, our economic and industrial history since the French Revolution has been marked by a degree of cooperation and close connection (rootedness) between individuals – and related complex divisions of labour – that have now reached global proportions.

The currents that have informed our artistic history are similarly varied. For example, in the field of visual arts and painting, while uprootedness characterizes the works of a Picasso at some stages of his career, the works of Van Gough and Chagall are characterized more by a sense of interconnectedness. Chagall's work is explicitly informed by Jewish mysticism. Although there is no up nor down in many of Chagall's works, they do reflect a vision of an inter-connection between nature and culture, between human and non-human life. All dichotomies associated with Ferry's uprootedness are blended together in a rich and complex unity in Chagall's paintings. In architecture, the work of the great Spanish architect, Gaudi, and his naturalist predecessors, reflects a sense of interconnectedness, a harmony of culture and nature.

Ferry's uprootedness, or sense of alienation, has contributed to a deep unhappiness, and languishing in humans – a sense that life is at worst awful, and at best unsatisfactory. This sense of uprootedness is hardly worth glorifying, and modern Biology indicates its delusory nature anyway.

Fascism and Nazism were themselves based in a sense of uprootedness. These regimes were deeply based in a delusory sense of separation. The evils of Nazism were only possible because Nazis felt a deadly sense of separation and alienation from Jews, Gypsies, gays, blacks and so on. If Nazis had a sense of connection with all of humanity and with nature instead of a deeply insecure attachment to "Aryan" culture, they could not have perpetrated the atrocities that characterised their brief but disastrous tenure. Human flourishing and happiness depends on a far more inclusive sense of connection than was achieved by the fascists and Nazis.

Luc Ferry continues

> "The antihumanism of these movements, which was explicit on a cultural level, was accompanied by a concern for rootedness that lent itself to the development of great attraction to ecology. To parody Marcel Gauchet's felicitous phrase, "the love of nature" (poorly) concealed "the hatred of men"". [253]

If we love nature, and if we see human beings as part of nature, then we must love humans. It is only possible to love nature and hate humanity if we see humans as separate from nature.

Human flourishing and ethics

Biology can help us develop a sense of connection, necessary for us to flourish. But biology is not enough. A mere intellectual acknowledgement of our connection with all living systems is not sufficient for our flourishing. We need to feel that sense of connection viscerally to flourish as human beings.

We need to use our understanding of these biological facts and hold it up as a mirror to ourselves and to reflect deeply on what implications these facts about our identity have for how we should live.

To feel that inclusive sense of connection with all living systems that is necessary to human flourishing, viscerally, it is necessary to live an ethical life. The development of a visceral sense of connection to all living systems requires that we develop a reverence for all life, and a disposition not to harm any living system unnecessarily. To use Kantian terminology, the cultivation of a visceral sense of connection with all living systems necessitates treating all living systems as ends in themselves and not merely as means towards our own ends.

If we dispose ourselves to unnecessarily harming living systems, or to using them merely as a means towards our own ends, then we are blind to, or refusing to acknowledge, the purpose and intrinsic value permeating these living systems. We thus develop a sense of separation, or alienation, from them. To the extent that we feel alienated from other living systems, we suffer.

If, on the other hand, we revere all living systems, and dispose ourselves against unnecessarily harming them, then we may develop a visceral sense of connection with these living systems. Thus it is in our own self-interest – that is, it serves our own flourishing - to live an ethical life.

Self-interest (our flourishing) and ethics are not at all at odds with each other. Our flourishing depends on our having a visceral sense of connection with all living systems and this in turn depends on our living an ethical life.

Authentic Happiness

In his book *Authentic Happiness* US positive psychologist Martin Seligman identifies a number of different strategies to realize human flourishing – or lasting happiness. These include:

- satisfaction about the past – gratitude and forgiveness [254]
- optimism about the future [255]
- happiness in the present – savouring and mindfulness [256]

These strategies or voluntary variables as Seligman calls them involve cultivating a sense of connection with time (gratitude, optimism, mindfulness), rather than a sense of alienation from time (regret about the past, fear of the future, dwelling in the past or future and not engaging with the present). Seligman also believes human flourishing or lasting happiness can only be achieved by being aware of and cultivating six virtues:

- wisdom and knowledge
- courage
- love and humanity
- justice
- temperance
- spirituality and transcendence. [257]

He considers various routes (strengths) by which we can achieve these virtues. For example, strengths leading to the virtue of knowledge and wisdom include: curiosity/interest in the world; love of learning; judgment/critical thinking/open mindedness; ingenuity/originality/practical intelligence; social intelligence; and perspective. [258] Seligman believes that identifying, building and using these strengths in work, love and raising children, produces flourishing. [259]

Cultivating these strengths and virtues involves developing a sense of connection with the world (wisdom, knowledge and spirituality) with life (love and humanity, justice) and involves developing internal harmony (courage and temperance).

The extent of human flourishing varies with the extent of a sense of connection. The greater and more inclusive our sense of connection the greater will be our flourishing. If we have a sense of connection with our family we do well;

if we have a sense of connection with humanity we do better and if we have a sense of connection with all living systems and the Earth we do better again.

Negative emotions such as hatred, jealousy, envy, and anger are rooted in a sense of separation and a sense of superiority or inferiority to others. These emotions involve comparison of self and others. These negative emotions cause us much suffering and are disruptive of internal harmony. They are reflective of a small self barricading itself against a threatening world.

Positive emotions such as compassion, caring, and sympathetic joy (feeling joy at another's good fortune) depend on a sense of connection with others. These emotions are reflective of a big self reaching out to and connecting with others. These emotions tend to make us feel good – unlike the negative emotions. They contribute to internal harmony and peace. Our flourishing depends on cultivating positive emotions and on refraining from cultivating negative emotions. While attempts to repress or eliminate negative emotions – a form of violence towards one's self - are likely to result in the disruption of internal harmony, cultivating these emotions – feeding them as it were – is also likely to result in inner discord.

The bigger and stronger we are – the more connected to big and strong things – the more spacious our lives will be. The more spacious our lives are the greater the prospect of our inner harmony. A sense of connection and internal harmony go hand in hand.

Conclusion

In Chapter Three I argued that from the fact that all living systems are equally valuable, it follows that we should do no harm to any living system *except* as it is necessary to your own flourishing or the flourishing of those you care about. If human flourishing consists of getting what you want then the principle "Do no harm except as necessary to human flourishing" would be too permissive – it would amount to saying "Do no harm except as necessary to get what you want." However, human flourishing does not consist of getting what you want but getting what you need for good health. The principle "Do no harm except as necessary to get what you need for good health" is considerably less permissive, since we do not need (for our good health) everything that we might want. What we want is potentially unlimited. What we need for good health is limited, as I have suggested above. We should do no harm unless our physical and mental health is at stake.

For example suppose our consumption of food and energy cause direct or indirect harm to other living systems. In reflecting on how we should live, we should examine the following questions: Is consumption at this level necessary for our internal balance and a sense of connection? Could we achieve internal harmony and a sense of connection by less harmful means? Are we perhaps over-consuming? Are we consuming more than is necessary to achieve internal harmony and a sense of connection? Is some of what we consume disruptive of our own harmony and sense of connection? I am not suggesting the answers to these questions are always clear, but they provide a framework for thinking about how we should live.

A second problem with the account of ethics developed in Chapter Three is that it is based on the idea that all living systems are equally valuable. How can we account for the strong intuition that it is more seriously wrong to harm a human than a bacteria or an insect if all living systems are equally valuable? It is to this question that we turn in the next chapter.

Chapter Five: Morality

We should do no harm to any living system except as necessary to our own flourishing. This principle flows from the intrinsic value of living systems. But human beings have a stringent obligation to do no harm to their fellow humans, to work for their flourishing and to share the fruits of their collective endeavours. By 'obligation' I mean 'a binding requirement as to action' and also 'the state or fact of being indebted for a benefit, favour or service'. [260] These obligations flow from the fact that humanity has increasingly become over the last ten thousand years, and especially over the last hundred years, a collective survival enterprise [261] in which we all work together towards human survival and flourishing. Humanity has increasingly become a vast superorganism [262] – like a huge ant, bee or termite colony. A superorganism generates various obligations on its members – to do no harm, to help each other and to share. These special obligations do not arise from any greater intrinsic value of humans over other living systems but from the fact that humanity is increasingly a global collective survival enterprise – that binds individuals together. Whereas morality focuses on the obligations [263] arising from our social ties – promising, truth telling, fairness – ethics relates to more general questions about how one should live. [264]

Downward Causation

Living wholes regulate the behaviour of their parts. Superorganisms shape the activities of component organisms, organisms shape the activities of their component cells and cells influence the behaviour of their components including the genes. This process is called downward causation.

I will now discuss four examples of downward causation: from genome to gene; from cell to organelle; from multicellular organism to cell and from superorganism to component organism. The examples I give are of the whole regulating the reproductive, replicating and work activity of its components.

The reader may wonder what downward causation has to do with human morality. The answer is that morality arises from downward causation from human society to individuals.

The genome regulates genes

A gene is a unit of heredity. Genes are DNA sequences that can be replicated and passed on. Genes are linked together end to end to form chromosomes. A chromosome then is a long DNA molecule and some associated proteins. A genome is all the chromosomes in a cell. There are 46 chromosomes and between 20-30,000 genes in a human genome.

The fact that genes are linked on chromosomes restrains the reproductive/replicative activity of genes. When one gene is replicated they all are. This coordinated replication forces cooperation on genes. They are all in the same boat. [265]

For example, in mitosis, or cell division, each chromosome divides lengthwise into two chromotids which separate and form the chromosomes of the resulting daughter nuclei. All the genes replicate together in a coordinated way. Each daughter cell gets the same genetic material as the parent.

Genes have little prospect of independent replication within a multicellular organism because, almost always, complex multicellular organisms originate from a single cell that multiplies by mitosis.

But there are loopholes. There are various ways in which genes can 'cheat', gaining over-representation in future generations. [266] This is achieved not through mitosis but through sexual fusion and meiosis. [267]

- In plants, as in animals, mitochondria are transmitted only in the egg cell. Genes in the mitochondria of hermaphroditic plants can cause male sterility, thus leading a plant to direct more of its resources into producing seeds and so making more copies of itself. [268]
- Some genes can gain over-representation in future generations by meiosis. While most genes obey Mendel's laws and are not over-represented amongst gametes produced by an organism, one pair of genes produces a toxin that kills gametes not carrying that gene, while the other protects gametes carrying that gene from the poison. The

result is the genes are over-represented amongst off-spring [269]

There are strong selective pressures operating at the level of the organism and the species that limit such independent replication – or selfish genes.

A selfish element that is too successful at multiplying within a cell will kill its host and itself at the same time. This can cause selfish elements to evolve mechanisms to limit their own growth. It can also cause the genome to evolve such mechanisms. Organisms/species that evolve mechanisms that rule out certain kinds of selfish genetic behaviour are more likely to survive as organisms/species than those that lack such mechanisms. [270]

For most possible kinds of selfish gene, there are many more genes whose interests would be served by suppressing the selfish behaviour. Thus there are selective pressures for the genome to impose 'government' in the 'public interest' and suppress selfish behaviour. This is called the 'Parliament of the genes'.

The cell regulates organelles
Mitochondria are organelles that convert oxygen and nutrients into adenosine triphosphate (ATP). ATP is the chemical energy that powers the cell's metabolic activities. [271]

Today, it is generally accepted that mitochondria are descendents of formerly free living bacteria. [272] The evidence for this is that mitochondria

- multiply within a cell by binary fission [273]

- are around the same size as bacteria [274]
- have their own DNA (similar to the DNA of bacteria) which encodes 13 proteins essential for respiration [275]
- have their own ribosomes (cellular machinery for the production of proteins) and RNA. [276]

As we saw in Chapter One, it is hypothesized that millions of years ago small, free-living bacteria were engulfed, but not digested, by larger bacteria. Over time, the two organisms developed a symbiotic relationship, the larger organism providing the smaller with nutrients and safe lodgings, and the smaller organism providing the larger one with ATP molecules. [277]

The reproductive activity of mitochondria is regulated to an extent by the cell. The number of mitochondria present in a cell depends upon the metabolic requirements of that cell. That number may range from a single large mitochondrion to thousands of the organelles. Human liver cells have around 2,500 mitochondria and muscle cells several times that number. So the rate of reproduction of the mitochondria is tied to the energy needs of the cell in which they live. [278] It is interesting to note that mitochondria reproduce more rapidly in a cancer cell than in a healthy cell. Lynn Margulis and Dorion Sagan comment: "The symbionts fall out of line, once again asserting their independent tendencies, reliving their ancient past." [279] It also suggests that a healthy cell regulates the reproductive activity of its mitochondria.

The multicellular organism regulates its cells

Multicellular organisms (such as animals, fungi and plants) regulate the activity of the numerous cells that constitute their bodies. We have seen in Chapter One that a characteristic of multicellular life is *cellular harmony.* [280] In a healthy multicellular organism the cells cooperate with each other in harmonious ways in the interests of the whole. [281] There is a sense in which they *must* cooperate since like the genes in a genome or the organelles in a cell they are all in the same boat. They sink or swim together. [282]

A crucial aspect of the mutual dependence of cells on each other in a multicellular organism is the fact that each cell has a specialisation. The activities of the cells are organised into a combination of labour. In a human there are around 200 different types of cells [283] each with a specific function – such as muscle cells, nerve cells, skin cells, liver cells, heart cells and blood cells. These different cell functions are not attributable to each type of cell having a different complement of genes, since each type of cell, apart from germ cells, have identical genes inherited by mitosis from the fused sperm and egg cell.

Although each cell has the same complement of genes, different genes are switched on and they are expressed differently. When specialised cell types divide they transfer not only their genes to each daughter but also information concerning their acquired pattern of gene expression. In addition to the DNA is an additional level of patterning. It is this additional form of marking that distinguishes one cell type from another. [284]

Cells also receive signals from the body itself. For example embryonic skin cells near the region of the body surface where an eye will be formed are induced to change their expression so that what they turn into forms part of an eye lens. [285]

A multicellular organism limits the reproductive activities of its cells. This is necessary to achieve what Noble calls cellular harmony.

William Clark argues that single celled organisms are at least potentially immortal. Single celled organisms such as bacteria reproduce by fission. The cell replicates its own DNA and divides into two daughter cells each receiving one copy of the DNA. Clark argues

> *Thus the organism – the single cell – never truly dies.* After all, where is the body? Can there be death in the absence of a corpse? These cells are in effect immortal. [286]

Given protection from predators and enough food and space to grow, bacterial cells could continue reproducing in perpetuity.

While bacteria may be potentially immortal, the life of a free-living bacteria is, however, rather tenuous in practice. Clark notes

> An average bacterium is about one cubic micrometer in volume and can divide by fission in as little as thirty minutes. Simple arithmetic shows that sixty to seventy cell divisions later – less than two days after starting to divide – the progeny of a

single bacterium, if they all survived, would be roughly equal in biomass to all of the human beings presently on earth. [287]

Clearly not all bacteria survive to reproduce. Most starve.

If you are a living organism, a good strategy of self-maintenance is to become part of a multicellular organism or a superorganism.

The greatest advantage of being part of a multicellular organism or a superorganism is benefiting from a combination of labour.

Single celled organisms, such as bacteria, are, according to Clark, effectively immortal. Supply them with enough food and space to grow, and mitosis would proceed indefinitely. [288]

Not so all cells. There appears to be a very close connection between the specialisation of cells (in multicellular organisms) and their mortality. Thus human fibroblast cells – cells that help make scar tissue – if separated from the body and put into culture with an unlimited supply of nutrients, kept at body temperature, in a humid environment, begin mitosis. But eventually the rate of mitosis slows, and, after a time, stops altogether. A week or so after the final division the cells die.[289] On average, fibroblasts separated from a human foetus undergo 50 rounds of cell division outside the body before stopping. Fibroblasts taken from a middle aged person undergo 20-30 rounds of mitosis, and cells taken from an elderly person divide only a dozen or so times. [290]

Clark cites evidence that for a little while, all of the cells in a growing human embryo are immortal. It is not until the cells in the embryo begin to differentiate, or specialise, into nerve cells, muscle cells and so on that all of the cells in the embryo become mortal. [291]

Not all human cells are mortal. Cancer cells are immortal. For example, cells taken from a tumour of Henrietta Lacks (*HeLa* cells) in 1951, and cultured in laboratories throughout the world, have kept on dividing ever since. They long outlived poor Henrietta. Clark observes "the majority of tumours show almost no signs of cell specialisation; they have either "de-differentiated," or have arisen from a small pool of cells within each tissue that show limited degrees of differentiation." [292]

Cancer cells may be immortal, but as we know all too well, because of rapid division and the need for space to grow, they eventually kill their hosts and themselves in the process. As Clark notes "An immortal tissue in a mortal body is a recipe for disaster." [293] It might be added that an immortal tissue in a multicellular body is a recipe for disaster. It hardly seems surprising, then, that "somatic cells even have a number of safeguards built in to make sure they do not backslide and try to become immortal." [294]

Clark asks "But to whom or what are these programs advantageous?" He answers his question by saying that the "only answer possible, the only conceivable beneficiary, is the DNA being passed from the previous generation to the next generation." [295]But why should the DNA in my children care whether or not my somatic DNA lives on? How does the DNA in my child benefit from my

DNA being destroyed along with my body? Clark does not explain this.

A much more straightforward answer to the question "Who benefits from the mortality of our cells?" is "We do" and "Our cells do". We benefit from the mortality of our cells because as multicellular organisms, we cannot function for long as an integrated whole if too many of our cells are immortal. Immortal cells are much more suited to a solitary existence than being part of a multicellular organism. Immortal cells cannot accept the discipline, the specialisations that multicellular organisms require. They cannot cooperate with their neighbours well enough to be useful parts of a whole multicellular organism. They are renegades. If their mitotic division is unchecked they kill their hosts quickly.

Our cells benefit greatly by being part of a well-functioning multicellular organism. In animals, cells are bathed in intracellular fluid, kept out of direct sunlight, kept at an even temperature, and are constantly well fed. They are cosseted creatures compared to their single-celled cousins. They do not have to fend for themselves. In such luxurious conditions, immortal (or independently reproducing) cells would multiply uncontrollably. [296]

Any cell faces a Faustian bargain with respect to enjoying the protection of multicellular existence. To be a useful part of a multicellular organism, to enjoy the benefits that a combination of labour can bring, a cell must give up its independence, its autonomy, and, it appears, its immortality. It must accept stringent limits to its mitotic division.

Given that most terrestrial environments are uneven, it is difficult for a cell acting alone to eke out a living. Most single-celled organisms die anyway – from starvation or accident. Life for a single-celled organism is often short, brutish and nasty. A cell may benefit by cooperating with others, as part of a multicellular organism. The price of this easy and healthy existence is giving up independent reproduction and "immortality".

Superorganisms regulate the activities of component organisms

Peter Corning defines "Superorganism" as "a behavioural system (social system) in which there are interdependent, coordinated actions with respect to one or more collective, goal-related activities." [297] This definition is a broad one, including cooperative hunting behaviours amongst lions. These are "temporary" superorganisms. On this definition a club or organisation of any kind would be a superorganism.

I define superorganism more narrowly as a cooperative survival/reproductive enterprise characterised by an extensive division or combination of labour. Paradigm cases of superorganisms on this definition are social insect colonies such as ant, bee, and termite colonies. It would also include colonies of bacteria such as stromatolites and microbial mats, [298] colonies of algae such as volvocales, [299] colonies of mammals such as naked mole rats [300] and of course human societies. Organisations such as school systems are not superorganisms but rather organs of the social body – the analogue of the heart or lungs in an organism.

Superorganisms generate various ways of making a living for its constituents. Instead of occupying a niche directly within an ecosystem, as a solitary insect (such as a fly) does, a social insect occupies a niche as a specialist within a colony, contributing to the flourishing of the colony and the individuals within it. The colony itself occupies a niche within an ecosystem but the individuals within the colony occupy a niche within the colony. The solitary insect faces the world alone; social insects make a living together. And the solitary insect depends on no one for their survival (though they depend on each other for their reproduction. All insects are social to that extent). The social insect depends on a team to meet their needs.

We saw in Chapter One that whether a leaf cutter ant is a queen, a soldier, a forager or minima is unlikely to depend on different genes, but arises from the response of a similar genotype to different social circumstances. The different "castes" of a leaf cutter ant colony are likely to be induced by different diets, at any rate different chemical signals, to develop in different ways [301] according to the needs of the colony.

In most social insect colonies workers can switch tasks, so that at any one time the proportion of ants engaged in, say, foraging or caring for the young may change, according to the needs of the colony. [302] For example, in a colony of honey bees the proportion of bees foraging will depend on the amount of nectar in the hive. But to ensure organised task switching, environmental cues are not sufficient. Individual workers must communicate with each other. [303] Honey bee scouts can communicate to foragers the location of food sources (nectar) using a dance. If a scout finds a source of nectar within 100 metres of the hive, she will perform a round dance, first in one direction and then the other. The performance is a multi-media one, as the dancer brings with her some of the odour from the nectar. Scouts also mark the nectar with their own scent to aid identification of the source. [304]

If the nectar is over 100 metres away, the scout is able to inform would-be foragers of the direction and the distance of the food source for up to 4 kilometres from the hive. This is achieved by a figure eight dance, first in one direction and then the other. The figure eight has a long connecting line between the two circles – like two capital Ds joined back to back. The connecting line indicates the direction of the food source. Distance is conveyed by the speed of the dance along the connecting line. For example, if this part of the dance takes two seconds this tells the foragers the food source is half a kilometre away. If it takes 6 seconds, this indicates that the food source is 4 kilometres away. The foragers do not see how long the scout's dance along the connecting line takes. The dances are performed in relative darkness, inside the hive. Rather the scout waggles its abdomen producing a constant buzzing sound that foragers feel or hear. [305]

Work in social insect colonies is organised in a highly decentralised way and depends on local communication between individuals, rather than hierarchical organisation.

In all social insect colonies, the colony regulates the reproductive activities of individual members. A reproductive division of labour between fertile queens and drones on the one hand and non-fertile workers on the other is a common characteristic of most insect societies. This can lead to disharmony within insect societies. For example in honey bees some workers have functional ovaries. Although workers do lay eggs, these are usually destroyed by other workers. [306] If workers were allowed to reproduce, this would disrupt the finely tuned combination of labour within the colony.

Similarities between the four examples

There are some major similarities between these four examples of wholes regulating parts. There are similarities in these examples of the relationships between the parts similar to those we examined in Chapter One. In each example, the relationship between the parts can be characterised as cooperative and harmonious. This cooperation depends on communication between the parts and involves a combination of labour. The combinations of labour result in synergies. The parts of each whole are dependent on each other (*Obligate* to each other). Cooperation produces synergies, but it also creates interdependence and an individual stake in those synergies. [307] Each part is specialised for the role it plays in the "system". Each part is also completely dependent on the other part; no part could exist without the services of the others, and only together can they survive and reproduce successfully. [308] They 'must cooperate' since they are all in the same boat. [309]

Wholes are Self Regulating

Each of the systems we have considered - the genome, the cell, the multicellular organism and the superorganism are self regulatory systems. As Noble notes "Complicated systems generally tend to regulate themselves by feedback effects, that is, by a process in which higher level (systems) parameters influence lower level components".[310] This is the case in each of the four examples. Corning observes that functional differentiation requires *cybernetic regulation* – the parts must be coordinated to achieve the objectives of the whole. Synergies associated with functional differentiation (such as a combination of labour) create selective contexts that in turn favour the evolution of cybernetic regulatory mechanisms. [311] Corning postulates that wholes at various levels of biological organisation may evolve mechanisms that permit partially autonomous control over the parts and their actions. [312] This is apparent in our four examples – the parliament of the genes, the regulation of mitochondria, cell differentiation and task allocation in superorganisms.

This regulation is not overwhelming. Nor is power necessarily centralised with any particular component. As Noble notes "no one set of molecules is given position of privilege over another … there are no privileged components telling the rest what to do. There is rather a form of democracy, with every element at all levels having a chance to be part of a regulatory network". [313]

Wholes generate obligations

The whole generates obligations - Each part is specialised for the role it plays in the "system". Each part is also completely dependent on the other part; no part could exist without the services of the others, and only together can they survive and reproduce successfully. There *is* some wriggle room. We have seen there are cases of intragenomic conflict, cases of intraorganismic conflict such as cancer, and intra colonial conflict in social insects, but this is limited because there is selective pressure for systems to develop mechanisms to prevent selfish individuals and for individuals to curb their own selfishness.

What obligations do wholes generate on their parts? There are three obligations. First, wholes impose on their parts *an obligation to do no harm* – an obligation not to aggress against another part of the same system. This should not be too surprising. A living system in which the various parts are in conflict with one another would not be as healthy, and would not be as likely to reproduce as a system in which the parts do no harm to each other. A system in which the parts expend energy harming each other is likely to be less efficient than a system in which the parts are in harmony each other, since energy that could be directed towards achieving the objectives of the whole is diverted towards harming other individuals who also could be directing their efforts to achieving the flourishing of the whole. If the scale of the harm to others within the system becomes too great it may disrupt the functioning of the whole. Cancer cells multiply more rapidly than healthy cells resulting in destruction of surrounding healthy tissue. In many cases cancer kills the organism which feeds it, so eventually destroys itself. Recall that flourishing systems depend on teamwork. If a team is divided against itself then the overall performance of the team is undermined. It is small wonder then that systems evolve mechanisms to regulate activities of their parts that may be harmful to other parts.

Second, wholes impose on their parts an obligation to work towards the flourishing of the whole. To a greater or lesser degree, a system imposes on its parts a specialisation that is part of an organised labour process directed towards the flourishing of the whole. The whole creates employment opportunities, or allocates tasks for its parts, that are organised in such a way as to contribute to the flourishing of the whole. A leaf cutter ant colony creates employment opportunities for reproduction (filled by few individuals) cutting leaves, carrying leaves, pulping leaf material, gardening, waste disposal, defence, food distribution and nursing. All of these tasks are directed to the flourishing of the whole and other individuals in the colony. A leaf cutter ant has no choice but to make a living in one of these ways and little choice as to how she makes a living. She cannot choose to make a living for herself – to become a solitary insect. She must work with others for others. To this extent "altruism" is forced on her. In some social insect colonies individuals will switch tasks – but which tasks they do depends on the needs of the colony as a whole. A black ant may switch tasks throughout its life. But it has no choice about whether to work or not, or whether to work for others or itself, and little choice about which tasks it does. Similar comments apply to cells in a multicellular organism, organelles in a cell, and genes in a genome. This specialisation makes individuals completely dependent for their livelihood on other individual parts of the whole. Their flourishing, indeed their very survival, depends on the performance of the whole.

Third, wholes impose on their parts an obligation to share the fruits of their collective labour with each part of the collective. The fruits of collective labour are to be shared in accordance with need. In each of the four examples we considered, the fruits of the combination of labour are shared equally. For example, we saw in Chapter One that ant colonies have a "social stomach". When one ant is hungry they all are – to about the same degree. This conveys valuable information to colony members. When the colony requires a particular nutrient, the foragers require it too and so seek it without having to be directed by a central command. [314] All social insect colonies have some form of social stomach.

Colonies of single celled organisms – that is, multicellular organisms – also share water and nutrients equally between all component cells. Most animals have a circulatory system. In our own bodies the circulatory system includes the heart, blood vessels, blood, lymphatic vessels and lymph that together serve to transport such materials as oxygen, nutrients and waste products. Smaller animals have an open circulation. Blood is pumped into the body cavity in which the organs are suspended. Tissues are in direct contact with the blood and materials exchanged directly by diffusion. In closed circulation systems blood flows in vessels – veins, arteries, capillaries. Blood flows in one direction through a series of one way valves. But the overall effect is that each cell receives all the water and nutrients it needs – if not directly from a capillary then through extra-cellular fluid.

The cytoplasm of a cell is the substance that fills the cell. It is a jelly-like material consisting of eighty percent water and is usually clear in colour. The cytoplasm contains dissolved nutrients and helps dissolve waste products. The cytoplasm helps materials move around the cell by moving and churning through a process called cytoplasmic streaming. Cytoplasmic streaming transports nutrients, enzymes, and larger particles within cells and enhances the exchange of materials between organelles. Through such processes all organelles obtain access to needed nutrients.

The obligations imposed by living wholes on their parts can be summarised as:

- Do no harm to other individuals within the whole
- From each according to their ability
- To each according to their need.

In addition parts of wholes have an obligation to communicate with other parts accurately as a basis for cooperative action towards the good of the whole.

The nature of these obligations
In what sense do wholes generate obligations on their parts?

There are four senses in which wholes might be said to generate obligations on their parts to do no harm to each other and to cooperate with each other.

First, the parts are obliged to cooperate in the sense that they are *compelled or forced to do so*. This is frequently the case. Individuals within the whole often have no alternative but to cooperate with others. It is the way the whole is made that the parts cooperate with each other. However, this is not always the case. For example, multicellular organisms sometimes suffer cancer. Cancer cells do not meet their obligations to do no harm and to cooperate with other cells in the body toward the good of the whole. They do not accept a specialisation. Thus cells in a multicellular organism are not obliged to do no harm or to cooperate with others in the sense of being compelled or forced to do so – though no doubt multicellular organisms have evolved regulatory mechanisms to prevent cancer.

Second, the parts are obliged to cooperate in the sense that they are *regulated to do so*. Individuals within living wholes are obliged to cooperate with each other because there are rules (regulatory mechanisms) in place against not doing so. We have seen that living wholes regulate the activities of their parts. In this sense Australians over the age of 18 are obliged to vote, but sometimes they do not. Obligation in this sense is similar to a legal obligation, but instead of being against some law or other, non-cooperation with other parts is against certain regulations of the living whole. The living whole regulates against non-cooperation.

Third, the parts are obliged to cooperate in the sense that *the flourishing of the whole* and therefore the inter-dependent parts are *conditional upon cooperation between the parts*. The parts *must* cooperate if the team is to flourish or even survive. Noble notes that "in a healthy organism [the cells] must cooperate in harmonious ways in the interests of the whole, despite the fact they have their own 'selfish' interests which, if given free rein, lead to diseases like cancer. I say 'must cooperate' since like the genes... 'they are all in the same boat'. However the cooperation has arisen, it is necessary." [315] But necessary for what? Cooperation is necessary for the flourishing of the whole and each of the co-dependent parts. It is rarely the case, however, that the flourishing of the whole depends on the cooperation of each and every part. A tree can survive the death of a leaf, or even the loss of a branch. The loss of a branch on a tree may have little impact on the roots, or other branches. In an animal the loss of an organ or a limb would be more severe than the loss of a cell.

Fourth, the parts are obliged to cooperate in the sense that *they owe a debt of gratitude to the other parts*. Any individual part of a living whole flourishes as a result of the team effort of all other individuals. If the efforts of an individual do not directly benefit another, they will indirectly do so. It would be an inappropriate response to the efforts of the team for an individual not to pull their weight – and in some cases to get a free ride and in others to imperil the performance of the whole team.

Human Superorganisms

In common with ants, termites and bees, individual humans are part of vast superorganisms – even a planet size superorganism. For we belong to vast cooperative survival/reproductive enterprises characterised by an extensive division or combination of labour. Of all superorganisms, human superorganisms have the most specialisations in nature. Humans divide their labour in many more ways than any other species. There are a bewildering number of ways human beings can make a living – occupations that humans can, within limits, choose. Most of these occupations are involved with the provision of goods and services to others, contributing to the flourishing of other humans and of human society.

It has not always been thus. For tens and thousands of years human societies resembled those of their relatives – chimpanzees and bonobos. Humans lived in fairly small and dispersed bands with limited division of labour – perhaps a simple gender division of labour. It took the invention and widespread adoption of agriculture and animal husbandry to generate the food surpluses necessary to sustain a wider range of ways of making a living. It took the industrial revolution to create the energy surpluses necessary to sustain the divisions of labour characteristic of today's societies. The invention of writing and much later the printing press, and more recent advances in information and communications technology, facilitated the kind of mass communication necessary to refine the organisation of labour and production processes necessary to the extraordinary flowering of occupations characteristic of human societies today.

Contemporary human societies much more closely resemble insect societies than the societies of our nearest non-human relatives – the chimpanzee and the bonobo. Contemporary human societies are a peculiar hybrid resembling insect societies in their specialisations and combinations of labour but having hierarchies more reminiscent of chimpanzee societies. It would appear that human societies have evolved so rapidly into a vast superorganism that we have not been able to leave behind ways of life that we picked up from living in small bands. Gender divisions of labour that we see today may be a legacy or a hangover of these older ways of life.

Economically we live in a highly globalised world. Because of refinements in transport and communication technologies over the past few centuries, human individuals participate in an increasingly global combination of labour. Goods and even some services made in one country may be transported around the world. Increasingly many of us work for and collaborate with individuals who live on different continents. Many businesses are global in scale or work closely with other businesses in diverse parts of the world. Many not-for-profit organisations are also global in scale such as Greenpeace or the World Wildlife Fund. Interestingly, world religions – collective meaning making enterprises – are commonly globalised, whether through colonisation, conquest or global migration.

Politically the world is not as globalised. The nation state is still strong and people tend to identify with it more closely than with the world economy. There is no world government as such, though organisations such as the United Nations are global decision-making forums.

Individual humans then are part of a bigger whole – super humanity. That whole is a super organism. Previously I analysed and compared the relationship between parts and the living whole at four different levels: the genome; the cell; the multicellular organism and the superorganism. Do the comments I made about the similarities in the relationship between part and whole at these levels extend to the relationship between humans and superhumanity?

Cooperation and Harmony

Relationships between humans in human society are by and large harmonious and cooperative. But what of the wars between humans? As Anthony Grayling observes "…it is easy to see that the peaceful and constructive things humans do far outweigh the negative things they do. Proof: look at the cities of Europe. They took centuries to build. They contain theatres and libraries, bookshops and galleries, sewage systems and paved roads, schools, post offices, hospitals, homes with furniture and comforts for the great majority. None of this took a day or a week to make; it took centuries of civilisation and culture. And this means that it took centuries of cooperation, agreement, discussion, forethought and stability. Europe abounds in cities; not even the tonnages of high explosives and incendiaries that rained down on them during the 1940s interrupted them for long, despite the terror and ruin caused." [316]

Combination of Labour
Human societies are characterised by the most extensive combinations of labour in nature.

The US Department of Labour identifies 23 major **groups** of occupation:

- Management
- Business and Financial Operations
- Computer and Mathematical occupations
- Architecture and Engineering
- Life, Physical, and Social Science Occupations
- Community and Social Services
- Legal Occupations
- Education, Training, and Library
- Arts, Design, Entertainment, Sports, and Media

- Healthcare Practitioners and Technical
- Healthcare Support
- Protective Services
- Food Preparation and Serving Related Occupations
- Building and Grounds Cleaning and Maintenance
- Personal Care and Service
- Sales and Related Occupations
- Office and Administrative Support
- Farming, Fishing, and Forestry
- Construction and Extraction
- Installation, Maintenance, and Repair
- Production Occupations
- Transportation and Material Moving
- Military-Specific Occupations. [317]

Within each major group there are sub-groups. For example, within the education, library and training major group there are five sub-groups: Postsecondary Teachers; Primary, Secondary, and Special Education School Teachers; Other Teachers and Instructors; Librarians, Curators, and Archivists; Other Education, Training, and Library Occupations

Clearly there are thousands of ways of making a living in human society. And the US Department of Labour lists only the legal ones.

Synergies

Cooperation in human societies has massive payoffs. In the first chapter of his brilliant book *The Sacred Balance*, David Suzuki writes:

> Like any other species, human beings have survived because we possess certain traits that have helped us secure a place on Earth. We are not distinguished by an armoury of weapons such as quills, fangs or talons, nor are we possessed of exceptional speed, strength or agility. Our sensory acuity cannot compete with other animals; we cannot hear as well as a bat, smell as well as a dog or see as well as an eagle. Yet not only have we survived, we have flourished within a remarkably brief time on the evolutionary scale. The key to our success is the possession of the most complex structure on Earth: the human brain. [318]

I beg to differ with Suzuki on this point. At least one key to our success is our sociality and, in particular, our complex combinations of labour. Tremendous advances have been made in the sciences, technology, medicine, the arts and the humanities since the combination of labour enables individuals to specialise in these fields, devoting their lives to these creative pursuits, and sharing the fruits of their labour with their fellows. The combination of labour enables specialists to devote their careers to teaching, for example, that directly benefits the well-educated individuals as well as building human capital for the benefit of all members of society.

Dependency

In contemporary human societies, individuals are dependent on others for meeting their needs. It is doubtful whether humans could live, much less flourish, separated from human society. We tend to be specialists rather than generalists. We depend on other specialists producing the goods and services that we need to survive and to flourish.

Humans have the following needs, or requisites for integrated effective functioning:

- thermoregulation
- waste elimination
- nutrition
- water
- mobility
- sleep
- respiration
- communications
- social relationships. [319]

Obviously we depend on others for communication and social relationships. Most of us will depend on specialist energy suppliers, cloth and clothing manufacturers, builders and electricians, to meet our needs for thermo-regulation. Most, at least in the West, depend on sewage systems designed, built and maintained by other specialists for meeting our waste disposal needs. Even in countries without extensive sewage systems, specialists work to remove and process waste. Most of us depend on specialist others for meeting our nutritional needs. Very few of us would grow, harvest and prepare all of our own food. Even those that do would depend on techniques developed and refined by others down through the centuries.

Human societies generate obligations. To the extent that our obligations to each other are invented they were invented collectively. For example, no individual invented the law. Laws are all generated at the social level. The human superorganism generates certain obligations on each individual.

These obligations include:

1. Do no harm to other individuals within the whole
2. From each according to their ability
3. To each according to their need.

Do no harm

All societies have strict laws against harming human beings. For example, in all human societies killing a human being is prohibited, except in very unusual circumstances. We may kill a non-human organism for food. We may never kill a human for food. These obligations to each other are a component of every religious tradition. These obligations are generated at the collective or social level. No one (not even Moses) invented the laws against murder.

From each according to their ability

The human social body generates a myriad of employment opportunities. There are no ways for a human to make a living that are not generated by the social body – the human superorganism. The combination of labour and the way in which labour is organised is arrived at collectively rather than being the brain child of isolated geniuses. These employment opportunities are generated by the social body to meet the needs of that body and its component parts – individual humans. A way of making a living cannot arise if there is no need for it – if it does not serve some purpose in terms of the overall needs of a society or its members. Individuals in human societies are obliged to work if they are able to, because of the link between work and payment. Even a person who is unemployed is generally regarded as being part of the labour force. There are numerous laws surrounding ways of making a living – for example industrial relations laws regulating wages and conditions. Laws also regulate the establishment and conduct of a business. Individual humans may choose their way of making a living but always within this framework.

To each according to need

The human social body regulates distribution of the products of the combination of labour – goods and services in accordance with need. First, individuals are paid for their contribution to the combination of labour. Thus the fruits of the combination of labour are shared with those who contribute to them. Second, individuals are often taxed on the income they receive in exchange for labour or the profits from capital or the money they spend, and this is spent on provision of goods and services such as health care, education, and welfare. Taxation is commonly progressive so that those who earn more pay more.

The famous Harvard political philosopher, the late John Rawls, implied that a system of cooperation in human societies generates obligations (or rights and duties in Rawls' terminology) and underlies ideas of justice and fairness in distribution of resources. He wrote:

> The fundamental organizing idea of justice as fairness...is that of society as a fair system of cooperation over time, from one generation to the next. [320]

He identified three elements of the idea:

1. Cooperation is distinct from merely socially coordinated activity, for example, from activity coordinated by some central authority. Cooperation is guided by publicly recognized rules and procedures that those cooperating accept and regard as properly regulating their conduct.

2. Cooperation involves the idea of fair terms of cooperation: these are terms that each participant may reasonably accept, provided that everyone else likewise accepts them. Fair terms of cooperation specify an idea of reciprocity: all who are engaged in cooperation and who do their part as the rules and procedure require, are to benefit in an appropriate way as assessed by a suitable benchmark of comparison... Since the primary subject of justice is the basic structure of society, these fair terms are expressed by principles that specify basic rights and duties within its main institutions and regulate the arrangement of background justice over time, so that the benefits produced by everyone's efforts are fairly distributed and shared from one generation to the next.

3. The idea of social cooperation requires an idea of each participant's rational advantage, or good ...[321]

Justice as fairness is based on the principle that human individuals who work for the flourishing of others in a collective flourishing enterprise – are to benefit in an appropriate way. The benefits produced by everyone's efforts should be fairly distributed and shared.

Without a global government, redistribution policies across countries are decided in a decentralized manner by national governments, individual citizens and firms. Redistribution of income takes place through a variety of channels. The simplest and most direct instrument of international income redistribution is official development assistance. It is widely accepted that rich countries should contribute 0.7% of their gross national income to foreign aid.

In addition aid organisations collect funds from individuals through donation and indirectly through governments – through tax deductions on charitable donations.

It would be fair to say that distribution of goods and services on a global scale in particular falls some way short of being in accordance with need. Some individuals in the human survival enterprise have many more goods and services than necessary for their flourishing while others have much less than they need. To that extent the human social body is diseased. The disease is on a par with a circulatory disease in a human body. Circulatory disease, if untreated, can be fatal. So can too much inequality in the distribution of goods and services in human society – though the human social body seems remarkably resilient, perhaps because of the extraordinary degree of cooperation between individuals within the human social body.

An obligation to tell the truth

We have an obligation to be truthful. This is because the human flourishing enterprise requires effective communication between members. Deliberately lying to others undermines effective communication. Lying is an inefficient use of energy – for it generally takes more energy to successfully deceive others than it does to tell the truth. [322] Successful deception requires constant vigilance, lest the deception be discovered. It requires remembering whom one told what to, when. Honesty is the best policy. It takes less effort to be truthful than to deceive, effort that could be devoted to pursuing the public good. The smooth functioning of a collective flourishing enterprise requires good communication between members and good communication requires a high degree of trust and honesty. Thus it is not surprising that human societies have regulatory mechanisms aimed at promoting truth telling.

An obligation to keep our promises

We have an obligation to keep our promises. Much human good hinges on the possibility of binding another's will through a promise or other contract. Any exchange of goods and services depends on this. [323] Exchange, trade and organised markets are vital in facilitating the success of a collective flourishing enterprise. Exchange, trade and markets are underpinned by honest dealing and trust as well as explicit rules, laws and policing. [324] The success of the human flourishing enterprise depends on the institution of promising and on individuals keeping their promises. Thus, again, it is hardly surprising that human societies have regulatory mechanisms to ensure that individuals are trustworthy.

Ethics and Morality

A distinction can be drawn between ethics and morality. According to Bernard Williams in his insightful analysis of ethics in *Ethics and the Limits of Philosophy,* ethics relates to the question posed by Socrates "How should one live?" – a question about the manner of one's life. Williams suggests that "Morality should be understood as a particular development of the ethical...It peculiarly emphasizes some ethical notions rather than others, developing in particular a special notion of obligation." [325] Williams believes that morality is distinguished by the special notion of obligation it uses – Williams calls it "moral obligation" - and by the significance it gives to it. Morality tends to reduce all ethics to obligation.

Richard Norman identifies three characteristics of morality – as distinct from ethics. The first feature is that morality is experienced by human beings as a set of external demands to which they must conform. Moral obligation is inescapable. [326]

The second feature of the narrow conception of morality is its self-denying character. "Morality" is typically thought of as a set of negative constraints which require one to forgo one's own interests for the sake of others. [327]

The third distinctive feature of the narrow conception of morality is its individualistic nature. Moral judgements tend to be focused on the moral status of the individual agent – on his or her moral merit. [328]As Williams notes "Blame is the characteristic reaction of the morality system. The remorse or self-reproach or guilt...is the characteristic first person reaction within the system..." [329]

Can the foregoing discussion help us to understand these features?

Ethics and morality have different sources. Ethics is a response to the recognition of intrinsic value, and its implications for how one should live. Recognising that a living system has intrinsic value, you should do no harm to it. Morality arises from norms (obligations of differing degrees) generated by the social body - thus the association of morality with obligation. Recognising the intrinsic value of a living system may not place you under an obligation in respect of that living system – you may not owe the system anything, nor does it force or compel you to act in any way - but you should do no harm to that living system.

Morality is a part of ethics – but not the whole of ethics. Morality has to do with the implications for how one should live arising from being part of a greater social whole. Ethics includes morality, but deals with for example the implications of intrinsic value for how one should live. The constituency of morality is human beings. The constituency of ethics includes human being but encompasses all living systems.

Ethics asks the question, "How should one live?" Morality asks a more specific question "What are our obligations to each other arising from the fact that we (humans) are part of a superorganism – a collective flourishing enterprise?"

Part of the answer to the question, "How should one live?" is that we should live in a way that is responsive to the value in all living systems. We should do no harm to any living system except as is necessary to our own flourishing, or the flourishing of those we care about, or the flourishing of the wider superorganism to which we belong – there being no less harmful alternative.

Part of the answer to the question "What are our obligations to each other arising from the fact that we (humans) are part of a superorganism – a collective flourishing enterprise?" is that we have an obligation to do no harm to each other (no exceptions), to cooperate in the collective flourishing enterprise working towards the flourishing of other members of that enterprise, and we have an obligation to share the fruits of the cooperative flourishing enterprise equally with all members. We also have an obligation to tell the truth and to keep our promises.

Morality is not invented by individuals but is developed collectively at the social level. Thus morality is literally external to the individual though internal to the social body to which individual humans belong. Morality is not written on tablets of stone. It is not brought down from the mountain. Rather, morality is the product of individual human beings living together in a social body.

Morality places pressure on individuals to cooperate with other individuals to serve the interests of the social body and all the parts of that body – for example, to participate in a division of labour providing services to others or to serve the public good. This explains the apparent self-denying nature of morality. It is worth remembering, however, that each individual benefits greatly by cooperating with others in a division/combination of labour.

Morality is individualistic to the extent that it involves placing obligations on individuals to cooperate with others and pursue the public good. To the extent that individuals internalize this morality, they may feel guilt if they do not meet its requirements.

Morality is a reflection of the fact that humans live and work together, cooperating with others in a social body. Humans have obligations to other humans that they do not have to non-human living systems – such as an obligation to work towards the flourishing of humans and the obligation to share. Humans also have an obligation never to do harm to other humans. This is not because humans have greater intrinsic value than non-humans, but because humans are members of a team – a collective flourishing enterprise – and this generates obligations. Just as ants have a stringent obligation to do no harm to other ants in the colony but no such obligations to a caterpillar for example, humans have an obligation to do no harm to each other – but no obligation to do no harm to other living systems. We ought not to do harm to any living system, but we have no obligation to do no harm. This may account for the power of our intuition that it would be more seriously wrong – morally – to harm a human than to harm a cat, a caterpillar, or a cotton plant, even though, I have suggested, all living systems are equally valuable. It is more seriously *morally* wrong to kill a human than a non-human, even though all living systems are equal.

Sick Superorganisms

The human superorganism is less than flourishing. While there are substantial pressures to meet the obligations imposed on individuals by being part of a super organism, the degree to which we meet these obligations is less than perfect. For example, despite the obligation to do no harm, we still fight wars. Despite the obligation to share, some individuals have more than they need to flourish while others go hungry. Within nations tax avoidance is still prevalent, and between nations trade barriers and low levels of foreign aid limit sharing between nations.

Thus the human social body is diseased. Parts of the social body too often harm other parts of the body. This is the equivalent in an individual human body of an autoimmune disease – a disorder of the body's defence mechanism in which an immune response is directed against its own tissues. Wikipedia revealingly defines "autoimmunity" as "the failure of an organism to recognize its own constituent parts (down to the sub-molecular levels) as *self*, which results in an immune response against its own cells and tissues." Wars within a social body could be seen as a failure of the social organism (or perhaps certain collectives within it) to recognise its own constituent parts as self. Tax avoidance, trade barriers, and less than generous foreign aid – or conditional foreign aid – is the equivalent of a circulatory disease in an individual human body.

Why is the human social body so badly diseased? One possible reason is that in evolutionary terms, human superorganisms – as I have defined them – have existed for at most 10,000 years. The human social body – the planet-sized superorganism – has been in existence for at most five hundred years and has consolidated as such more recently than that. Social insect colonies, by contrast, have been evolving for millions of years, multicellular organisms have been evolving for around 600-800 million years [330] and eukaryotic cells have been evolving for 1,700-2,000 million years. [331] Life on Earth (an extensive combination of labour between proteins and nucleic acids) has been evolving for 4,000 million years. [332]

I define the term "superorganism" as a cooperative survival/reproductive enterprise characterised by an extensive division or combination of labour. The development of extensive combinations of labour in human societies was only made possible by the development of agriculture and animal husbandry that began to emerge about 10,000 years ago.

The development of agriculture/animal husbandry are not likely to have relied on extensive combinations of labour, since animal domestication by humans is likely to have arisen partly from keeping wild animals as pets, and partly from wild animals learning to benefit from closeness to humans (through scavenging). Early phases of agriculture are likely to have involved people harvesting wild plants, and accidentally scattering (sowing) seeds in the process.

This resulted in artificial (if unconscious) selection of those animals and plants most useful to us, and their eventual deliberate domestication. [333]

Agriculture allowed greatly increased food production and storage. [334] Hunter gatherers had little or no stored food, no concentrated food sources such as an orchard. Most people in a hunter-gatherer group were engaged in finding and processing food. [335] There may have been a simple gender division of labour amongst hunter-gatherers between male hunters and female gatherers – but not a more extensive division of labour. Only agriculture could support a more extensive division of labour.

As Jared Diamond notes, in a Hunter-Gatherer society "there can be no kings, no full-time professionals, no class of social parasites who grow fat on food seized from others. Only in a farming population could contrasts between the disease-ridden masses and a healthy, non-producing elite develop." [336] Equally, as Diamond recognizes, "Farming undoubtedly made it possible to sustain full-time craftsmen and artists, without whom we would not have such large-scale art projects as the Sistine Chapel and Cologne Cathedral." [337] (This is not to suggest that great works of art had to await the development of agriculture. Magnificent galleries of Australian Aboriginal rock paintings at Ubirr and Norlangie in Kakadu National Park in Northern Australia pre-dated the development of agriculture in Australia and probably the world.) Diamond is also correct to state that "when we count up the specialists whom society became able to support after the advent of agriculture, we should recall not only

Michelangelo and Shakespeare but also standing armies of professional killers." [338]

For good or ill, or a mixture of the two, agriculture/animal domestication enabled the extensive combination of labour that characterizes human superorganisms. Human superorganisms have been evolving for only 10,000 years at most. Compared to other superorganisms, human superorganisms are extremely immature. In comparison with insect colonies, and colonies of cells, they are only just beginning to emerge.

While connections between human superorganisms have been developing slowly for thousands of years, integration of the economies (and so combinations of labour) of these superorganisms on a global scale has occurred only very recently with improvements in transportation technology (ocean-going boats, horsepower, planes, trains and automobiles), infrastructure (roads, ports, airports) and communications technology (postal services, telephones, e-mail). Improvements in food storage technology have facilitated global trade in food. Thus some regions can specialise in food production, while others can specialise in finance. English is slowly becoming a global language and this has facilitated the integration of human superorganisms into a giant global human superorganism. Oil and coal energise this integration of human superorganisms.

So the emergence of the globe-sized human superorganism was very recent indeed.

A second reason for disease within human social bodies (especially inequalities) is hierarchies – such as class and gender. For much of human history, humans lived in small bands – consisting of five to eighty people – an extended family or several related extended families. [339] Bands are tiny societies in which divisions of labour or economic specializations are limited to those based on age and gender. [340] Band organisation tends to be informal and egalitarian, though some band members are looked up to by others on the basis of age, personality, strength and wisdom and these individuals tend to contribute more to decision making. [341]

In the transition from living in bands to superorganisms – marked by extensive divisions of labour – humans carried the old forms of band organisation with them, but in their new social context gender division of labour transformed into oppression of women and the simple differences in esteem of some became class hierarchies. Women became reproductive and child caring specialists. Specialisation in leadership – leaders and followers, bosses and workers, lords and serfs, masters and slaves – emerged. Aspects of social organisation became highly centralized.

There is no reason why superorganisms must be characterized by centralized forms of power relationships. Indeed, typically they are not. The organisation of social insect societies, for example, is decentralized. There are no rulers in insect societies. The so called "queen" is a reproductive specialist. There may be specialised "workers" but no bosses. Human superorganisms evolved differently because humans and their non-human ancestors were social animals long before they became parts of superorganisms, and they carried some of their old forms of organisation with them into the new forms of organisation. In their new context they were inappropriate and became distorted into social diseases – specifically social hierarchies of class and gender. The result is that within human superorganisms, divisions of labour have become gendered, and hierarchical (we have specializations in leadership and power). In turn, this results in gender and class inequalities. Those groups towards the top of the hierarchies are able to secure a greater share of resources than those at the base.

To compound the problem, these inequalities come to be seen as somehow inevitable and natural. How else could human societies be organised? We forget that human societies are aberrant in being, in part at least, centrally organised. Specialisation and division of labour are not aberrant of course. They are a common form of organisation at many levels of life – from cells, through multicellular organisms to insect societies. What is unusual is for specializations and division of labour to become overlaid with forms of social organisation more appropriate to small bands.

It might be argued that inequalities is the distribution of resources necessary to meet our needs occur because unlike social insect colonies human societies lack a "social stomach". Humans, however, possess a social stomach. Most of us are empathic to some degree and have a strong sense of justice. Our empathy, on the other hand, tends to be stronger for people "like us" than for "the other". As Anthony Grayling notes "It is clear that left to itself, the sympathy for which most of us have a natural capacity tends to be parochial. We put those close to us before those remoter from us..." [342] And we put those who are like us before those who are not like us, whether they are down the street or across the world. In other words, we put the "in-group" before the "out-group".

To the extent that we tend to identify with an in-group – see membership of that group as constitutive of whom we are – we may feel threatened by those who are members of an out-group. Their very existence may challenge our sense of who we are. In extreme cases we might be willing to fight for our beliefs. The tendency to identify at the level of the human sub-group rather than at the level of humanity or life itself might account for the fact that, as Grayling observes, "politically, human beings have advanced little in their long evolutionary history of conflict. They are still tribal, territorial and ready to kill one another for beliefs, and for control of goods and resources." [343] Political maturity may lie in the realization that we are all in the same boat – part of a global collective flourishing enterprise. It may lie in our identifying with humanity – or even better with life as a whole - rather than with a sub-group of humanity – a nation, a religion, or a tribe.

Conclusion

We have moral obligations to human beings that we do not have to other living systems. These obligations arise not from any greater value of humans compared with other living systems. These obligations – such as to never do harm, to share resources, to tell the truth, and to keep promises - arise from the human superorganism. No wonder we believe that it is more seriously morally wrong to harm a human being than to harm an insect or a tree.

We have no moral *obligation* to do no harm to an insect or a tree.

However, trees, insects and humans are (equally) valuable. This has implications for how we should live. We should do no harm to any living system, except as necessary for our own flourishing or the flourishing of those we care about. We are not obliged to trees and insects as we are to humans – but we should do no harm to them. The requirements of morality and ethics arise from different sources – the former from the human superorganism, the latter from the value of living systems.

Conclusion

To conclude I will posit some answers to life's big questions – the first about the nature of life itself.

What is life?

Life is *matter with intrinsic purpose*. It is characterised by organisation for an intrinsic purpose.

What is the purpose of life?

The purpose of life is to survive – that is, to live, live well and live better and to contribute to the continuation of one's lineage. This purpose is embodied in all living systems.

Many biologists think that the ultimate rationale for the existence of living beings is to reproduce and propagate genes. Richard Dawkins claims that our genes – the descendents of ancient replicators - "are in you and me; they created us, body and mind; and their preservation is the ultimate rationale for our existence." [344] William Clark claims that "In terms of the basic process of life itself, which is the transmission of DNA from one generation to the next...[our ability to think, feel, love and write] is just so much sound and fury, signifying certainly very little and quite possibly nothing." [345]

The view that the preservation of our genes is the ultimate rationale for our existence implies that genes created us – they confer purpose on cells, organisms and superorganisms. It implies that we are vehicles for the continuation of our genes and that we are survival machines for our genes. But we have seen that living wholes confer purpose downwards to their parts and outwards to the requisites for their continued existence. We confer purpose on our genes - they are tools we use to facilitate the production of proteins and for reproduction. Our genes do not confer purpose on us – we confer purpose on them.

The basic process of life itself is cooperation towards living, living well and living better. In humans, processes such as thinking, feeling, loving and writing are a significant part of living well and living better - the ultimate rationale for our existence.

Do we have a free will?
Yes. All living systems are organised for purposes. Living systems are not machines; they have purposes of their own. That is, living systems are self determining or autonomous, within limits. This freedom does not imply that living systems defy the laws of physics. Rather they harness the laws of physics to their own ends or purposes. [346]

What is the purpose of death?
To regenerate, refresh and renew life.

One major strategy for living systems to maintain their flourishing is to constantly make and re-make themselves.

Living systems continuously self-repair. The internal balance of a living system is maintained dynamically by the system constantly breaking down and replacing its components. This process of self-making requires an orderly flow of energy and matter through the system. It requires the intake of energy and matter by the system, production and repair of structural components and the elimination of material and energetic wastes – in a word, *metabolism*.

Cells maintain themselves by breaking down and reconstituting their macromolecular components. The proteins, nucleic acids and lipids are constantly being broken down and replaced by other more or less identical molecules. The life span of a protein molecule in a human cell is on average two weeks.

Multicellular organisms maintain themselves by replacing cells in their bodies. Each human cell has its own lifecycle from mitosis to death and replacement. Human cells have a lifecycle varying from a few days, through a few weeks to months.

This process of self-maintenance through constant replacement of living components is visibly apparent in the case of deciduous trees. Each autumn all the leaves of a deciduous tree die, to be replaced in the spring with new leaves. All trees shed their leaves replacing them with new ones over the course of their lives.

A similar strategy occurs at different levels of organisation. Individual ants are the counterpart to cells of a multicellular organism or the macromolecules of a cell. The colony maintains itself by generating new components – individual ants - and replacing old ones.

A lineage of organisms, that is, a species - maintains itself by constantly generating new components, new members of the species replacing old components.

The process of death and reproduction of members of species is analogous to the breaking down and replacement of cells in a multicellular organism or the breaking down and replacement of macromolecules in a cell. It appears to serve similar purposes.

Death is an integral part of the process of life. The components of all living systems are dying and being re-born constantly. Birth is not an event that occurs at the beginning of life, and death at the end of it. Birth and death occur constantly throughout our lives. Death is a means of re-generating and renewing life.

Life and death are interpenetrating processes. Death is part of, and programmed into, multicellular life. Death reminds us that we are part of a bigger whole beyond culture – part of the natural cycle of life and death. If we see culture as separate from nature we will be prone to see death as foreign to human life, imposed from without. Such a view appears to rest on a dichotomy between life and death, the immortal mind and the mortal body, culture (with its pretensions to immortality) and nature.

Biology can assist us to develop a greater sense of connection with all living things, and with nature. It can also help us to overcome our sense of alienation from death and allay our fear of death.

What is the colour of the living world?

The living world is green in stem and leaf not as is often claimed red in tooth and claw. The basic process of life is cooperation, not competition. Cooperation (organisation for a purpose) pervades the living world. But why should so many people, especially biologists, not notice the pervasiveness of cooperation in life? There are many reasons.

1. Cooperation in life is often invisible. Cooperation in life is most pervasive between components of cells within cells and between cells within multicellular organisms. Such processes are not visible to us. Ant, termite and bee societies are hidden from human view inside nests.

2. The vast cooperation between humans within human society may not be visible for a very different reason. It is so pervasive that our attention may not be drawn to it. Just as a fish swimming in the ocean may not even notice the water, but just take it for granted, so human beings swim in an ocean of cooperation that we simply take for granted. We are more likely to notice conflict, for that is dramatic and out of the ordinary. We, story making animals, find the vast cooperation of everyday social existence somewhat passé. Good stories need conflict, and/or strife and growth in the face of adversity.

3. Predatory relationships between organisms within an ecosystem also stand out against a background of vast majority of peaceable and cooperative relations. They stand out because of their importance in sustaining the flow of energy and

nutrients through an ecosystem. Predatory relations may seem so significant that the more numerous peaceable relations may not seem like relations at all. We notice the small competitive figure, but lose sight of the vast cooperative ground.

4. Ideas about free market capitalism and evolutionary theory arose at the same time and in the same place. No doubt theories of life and living processes were shaped by prevailing economic theories. No doubt too, some biologist sought to justify or naturalise prevailing political arrangements. As Karl Marx noted "Darwin recognises among brutes and plants his own English society with its division of labour, competition, opening up of new markets, inventions and struggle for existence." [347]

5. The theory of evolution was being developed at the same time and place as some deeply pessimistic views about life. For example, in the late 19th Century Frederick Nietzsche advocated the view that the more we know about reality the more frightful we realise that it is. Nietzsche revered the great Greek tragedians, Aeschylus and Sophocles for their courage in recognising the terrible nature of existence and yet affirms it in aesthetic terms. He saw nature as devoid of purpose and value. He writes "Think of a being such as nature is, prodigal beyond measure, indifferent beyond measure, without aims or intentions, without mercy or justice, at once fruitful and barren and uncertain..." [348] Modern biology emerged in an era where such a view of nature was widespread, at least in philosophical circles.

What is the source of value?

The history of western ethics has revolved around a debate between two views about the source and nature of value. According to the humanist view, the source of all value is humanity – value is rooted in human nature, the human condition or human desires. The other view is transcendental. It locates the source of value outside the human realm in a transcendent source that imposes on humanity the requirement to aspire to ends located beyond the physical world, commonly in a life after death. I have argued that neither of these views is correct. The source of value is not (exclusively) human but nor is it transcendental. The source of value is not humanity or the gods but life.

When did value come into the world?

Many thinkers would date the arrival of values with the arrival of humanity – no more than 300,000 years ago – and possibly with the development of language, perhaps around 100,000 years ago. I have argued for a much earlier origin of value. Good and bad came into the world with the first living system – around four billion years ago. The first living system – a microbial speck – would have had a state of health, good or bad, was capable of being benefited or harmed, and so had needs – requisites for flourishing. So the common view that values came into the world with humanity is wide of the mark by about four billion years.

Are values a part of the fabric of the world?

Yes. Values are a part of the fabric of life and so a part of the fabric of the world.

Can something be valuable without being valued?

Yes.

There would appear to be two ways something can be valuable. It can be valued or it can be value-able. Being valued is a source of extrinsic value. Being value-able is also a source of intrinsic value. If a living system confers extrinsic value on something then that system must have value, for how can one bestow upon anything that which one does not have?

All living systems are value-able and hence valuable. Living systems are good for something, that is, they are valuable. But they may or may not be valued by other living systems.

If values are objective why do people still do unnecessary harm?

If values are objective or real, as I have been arguing, why do these objective values not impact on or constrain people who do wanton harm to other living systems? Although they are real not everyone perceives objective values – and in particular the value in living systems. People may perceive something but not notice it. We sometimes do not notice something we are staring right at.

For example, we are surrounded by wonders that we seldom really notice because our minds are far away and we are not paying full attention. "Look at these tender leaves caressed by the sunlight. Have you ever really looked at the green of the leaves with a serene and awakened heart? This shade of green is one of the wonders of life. If you have never really looked at it please do so now." 349 So the Buddha counselled some young men troubled by the theft of some of their possessions. The young men grew very quiet we are told.

Are humans more valuable than other living systems?

I have argued they are not. All living systems are of equal value since they are equally alive, equally purposeful and organised equally well for the same purposes – to live, live well and live better. Living well may amount to something different for a bacterium, a bird, a fish or a human being. But this does not amount to a difference in value.

So why do we think that humans are more valuable than other living systems?

Perhaps it is because humans have obligations to each other as members of a society that they do not have to other living systems. But these obligations do not arise from any greater value on the part of humanity but from the fact that cooperative survival enterprises generate obligations on their members.

It could also be because of an attachment to an outmoded religious idea – the Great Chain of Being – that not just human society but the cosmos is ordered hierarchically from God in heaven (the Cosmic King or CEO) through angels to Man, the animals and plants. Some versions of the Great Chain of Being have fine distinctions between the value of living beings based on their apparent complexity. More contemporary versions suggest that humans are a more evolved life form or more complex and so more valuable.

Hierarchical organisation is very rare in the living world. It seems confined to the human superorganism. Why then should the cosmos be organised hierarchically?

What is happiness?

Happiness is the experience of our own flourishing – that is, the experience or awareness of our internal harmony and a deep sense of connection.

How can happiness be achieved?

US psychologist Sonja Lyubomirsky in her "work in progress" on happiness proposes to test kindness, gratitude and optimism as strategies to lasting happiness. [350] To her three strategies I would add a fourth – mindfulness. Thich Nhat Hanh says that mindfulness is remembering to come back to the present moment or as the energy that brings us back to the present moment. [351] Gratitude reflects a sense of connection with the past; optimism reflects a sense of connection with the future and mindfulness reflects a sense of connection with the present. Thus happiness requires cultivating a sense of connection with time – living in the present moment rather than dwelling on regret of or nostalgia for the past and fear of the future. It also depends on kindness – reflecting a sense of connection with all living beings – past, present and future. At least part of kindness involves recognition of the value of a living systems and cultivating a determination to do no harm to living systems. If you cultivate kindness towards yourself you do well. If you cultivate it towards humanity you do better. If you cultivate it to all living systems you do better again.

Why be ethical?

Why, for example, should we do no harm to any living systems? From a self-interested point of view, why should I do no harm to any living system (beyond what is necessary to my flourishing?) A reason to do no harm is that doing unnecessary harm strengthens a sense of separation and alienation between one's self and others. Our flourishing depends on a sense of connection – recognition of the unity of all life. Deliberately harming others is disruptive of internal harmony – another condition of flourishing.

There are other reasons, (not related to our own self interest) why we should do no harm to living systems. One reason is that living systems are highly valuable. One should revere and protect that which is valuable.

Can a theist accept Eco-Ethics?

Can a theist, such as a Christian, Jew or Muslim, accept Eco-Ethics? A theist could well accept the conclusions of Eco-Ethics. Albert Schweitzer himself was a theist, and a proponent of a life ethic. A theist could believe that God created all living systems and that therefore they are sacred and should not be harmed unnecessarily. A theist could also believe that God created all living systems with free will or self determination. Thus they have intrinsic value and should not be harmed. A theist who believed that all living systems are equal and sacred in the eyes of God would be likely to accept Eco Ethics. On the other hand, a theist or an atheist who embraced the idea of the Great Chain of Being – a hierarchy of value – would be unlikely to accept a life ethic such as Schweitzer's. But the Great Chain of Being doctrine is not a necessary part of a theology.

What does Biology tell us about how we should live?

I have suggested it tells us a great deal.

Biology tells us that all living systems are permeated by purpose, and all possess intrinsic value. Given this, what should our attitude be towards life?

The appropriate attitude is reverence: respect tinged with awe; a sense of wonder. Richard Norman suggests that reverence is a response to the natural world as a whole, whereas respect is a response to individuals. However, because of the inter-being nature of living systems, and of living and non-living processes, the whole natural world, in all its wonder, is manifest in each living individual and even in the products of living systems. The wonder of it all is manifest in a tiny flower or a spider's web.

The view that reverence, awe and wonder only applies to the whole of nature may reflect a human adult point of view. Rachel Carson noted:

> Many children, perhaps because they themselves are small and closer to the ground than we, notice and delight in the small and inconspicuous. With this beginning, it is easy to share with them the beauties that we miss because we look too hastily, seeing the whole and not its parts. Some of nature's most exquisite handiwork is on a miniature scale, as anyone knows who has applied a magnifying glass to a snowflake. [352]

A sense of wonder and awe at life, and living systems, very often requires cultivation. But we would all have experienced it, especially as a child. As Rachel Carson observed:

> A child's world is fresh and new and beautiful, full of wonder and excitement. It is our misfortune that for most of us that clear-eyed vision that clear instinct for what is beautiful and awe-inspiring, is dimmed and even lost before we reach adulthood. [353]

A misfortune for us and a misfortune for life on Earth.

Carson suggests that cultivating a sense of wonder and awe involves "learning again to use your eyes, ears, nostrils and finger tips, opening up the disused channels of sensory impression." [354] This involves cultivating mindfulness about what you see, hear, smell, and touch. It involves learning to live in the present moment. Carson gives an excellent suggestion to cultivate a sense of wonder and awe at what one sees.

> One way to open your eyes to unnoticed beauty is to ask yourself "What if I had never seen this before? What if I knew I would never see it again?" [355]

This approach brings us into the present moment with what we are seeing. Of course we can ask these questions in relation to any of our senses.

Being social animals, humans learn together. Cultivating a sense of reverence and awe for all living systems has implications for all of our social processes for learning, from parenting, through schooling, to practicing the sciences, the arts and religion. Don Cupitt suggests he would rather "in our education we taught people to understand and love their senses and bodily life better... At the moment our education is still defective in the arts and the senses, we put so much emphasis on maths and the sciences, and relatively little on education of the eyes and the sense of sight and the sense of hearing." [356]

The sciences, as well as the arts, if taught well, can also be an education of the senses. Cupitt approves of the fact "that the emphasis in the sciences is now perhaps beginning to move away from the physics that dominated the 20th century to the biology that will dominate the 21st." [357] The study of Biology, as much as the study of the arts, can awaken in us a sense of wonder, a sense of awe, at all living systems.

Given that all living systems are equally valuable, what dispositions (for example desires) should we cultivate towards them? I have suggested that we (individually and collectively) should dispose ourselves to do no harm and also to do good. Is there any priority we should give these dispositions? Should one be stronger than the other? I believe so. Our disposition to do no harm should trump any disposition to do good. We *must* not harm any living systems. We *may* do good.

The requirement to do no harm to living systems, or more specifically, to harm living systems only to the extent necessary to our individual and collective flourishing, provides a framework within which we may do good. We should dispose ourselves to do good, but not by means that harm a living system.

Eco-Ethics supports an activist position:

- against war;
- against violence to humans under any circumstance except where necessary – there being no less harmful alternative - in self-defence;
- against violence to any living system, except where this is necessary – there being no less harmful alternative - for human flourishing;
- against land clearing except where necessary – there being no less harmful alternative - for human flourishing;

- against factory farming of animals;
- against excessive consumption by humans – consumption that harms living systems and is not necessary to human flourishing;
- for zero population growth (in humans);
- for greater equality between humans in terms of distribution of resources and power.

Such activism may be pursued, but only within the usual constraint that we should above all do no harm – for all life is valuable.

For the sake of our own flourishing and the flourishing of all Earthly living systems, we should tread more lightly, and more mindfully, on the Earth.

About the Author

Rob Stevens is a Research Manager in the New South Wales Department of Education. He has a Bachelor of Arts and a Master of Arts in Philosophy from Adelaide University and a Doctorate in Philosophy from Macquarie University. He also has a Masters of Education from Sydney University. Most of Rob's career has been in policy and research positions in public sector education organisations. Rob has written extensively in Philosophy and Education.

Rob has had a lifelong interest in Biology and Philosophy. Eco-Ethics is a synthesis of this.

Rob enjoys reading, walking, film and participating in Sydney's "café society". He initiated a long running non-fiction book club. He has long been part of the Lotus Buds (Buddhist) Sangha in Sydney. He lives with his wife, Tamara, and Zeno the cat in the inner west of Sydney.

References

Introduction

[1] Plato *Euthyphro* in *The Last Days of Socrates: Euthyphro; The Apology; Crito and Phaedo* translated with an introduction by Hugh Tredennick Penguin Books England 1954
[2] Plato *The Symposium* translated by Walter Hamilton Penguin Books, England, 1951 page 95
[3] Levine, George *Darwin Loves You: Natural Selection and the Re-Enchantment of the World* Princeton University Press, New Jersey 2006 pages 73-92
[4] Levine *Darwin Loves You* page 89
[5] Levine *Darwin Loves You* page 60
[6] Barnham "The Emergence of Biological Value" in Dembski, William A and Ruse, Michael (ed) *Debating Design: From Darwin to DNA* Cambridge University Press 2004 page 211

Chapter One: Purpose

[7] Thich Nhat Hanh *Old Path White Cloud: Walking in the footsteps of the Buddha* Parralax Press, Berkeley, California 1991 page 114
[8] By "system" I mean "an assemblage or combination of things or parts forming a complex or unitary whole" (Macquarie Dictionary) Living systems include cells, such as bacteria or amoeba, multicellular organisms such as animals, plants and fungi, superorganisms such as termite, ant or bee colonies, lineages of organisms and ecosystems such as coral reefs.
[9] Skutch, Alexander F *Harmony and Conflict in the Living World* University of Oklahoma Press: Norman, 2000, page 47
[10] Dawkins, Richard *The Blind Watchmaker* Penguin Books 1986 page 1
[11] Thomas, Peter *Trees: Their natural history* Cambridge University Press, Cambridge, UK 2000 page 7

[12] Stern, Kingsley R, Bidlack, James and Jansky, Shelly *Introductory Plant Biology* Edition 11, McGraw Hill, New York, New York 2008, page 34

[13] Corning, Peter A *Nature's Magic: Synergy in Evolution and the Fate of Humankind* Cambridge University Press, Cambridge 2003 page63-64

[14] Corning, Peter A *Holistic Darwinism: Synergy, Cybernetics and Bioeconomics of Evolution* The University of Chicago Press 2005 page 5

[15] Denis Noble *The Music of Life: Biology Beyond the Genome* Oxford University Press 2006 page 96

[16] Corning *Nature's Magic* page 27-28

[17] Maynard Smith, John and Szathmary, Eors *The Origins of Life: From the Birth of Life to the Origins of Language* Oxford University Press, Oxford 1999 pages 111-113

[18] Corning *Holistic Darwinism* page 3

[19] Corning *Nature's Magic* page 57

[20] Noble *The Music of Life* page 96

[21] Noble *The Music of Life* page 50

[22] Noble *The Music of Life* page 52

[23] Thomas *Trees: Their natural history* page 163-164

[24] Stephen Rose *Lifelines: Biology, Freedom, Determinism* Penguin Books, London, England 1998 page 139

[25] Tudge, Colin *The Secret Life of Trees: How they live and why they matter* Penguin Books, London, England page 271

[26] Stern, Bidlack and Jansky *Introductory Plant Biology* page 33

[27] Based on Capra, Fritjof *The Web of Life: A new synthesis of mind and matter* Flamingo: Harper Collins, London, England pages 159-164

[28] Freeman Dyson *Origins of Life* Revised Edition, Cambridge University Press, Cambridge 1999 page 7

[29] Noble *The Music of Life* page 7

[30] Dyson *Origins of Life* page 8 and Corning *Nature's Magic* page 48

[31] *Molecular Expressions Cell Biology: Mitochondria* http://micro.magnet.fsu.edu/cells/mitochondria/mitochondria.html

[32] Simon Conway Morris *Life's Solution: Inevitable Humans in a Lonely Universe* Cambridge University Press, Cambridge, United Kingdom 2003 pages 198-200

[33] Bert Holldobler and Edward O Wilson *Journey to the Ants: A Story of Scientific Exploration* The Belknap Press of Harvard University Press, Cambridge, Massachusetts, London, England 1994 pages 117-122

[34] Holldobler and Wilson *Journey to the Ants* page 118

[35] Conway Morris *Life's Solution* page 199

[36] Holldobler and Wilson *Journey of the Ants* pages 112-114

[37] Holldobler and Wilson *Journey to the Ants* page 46

[38] Holldobler and Wilson *Journey to the Ants* page 51 and 55

[39] Holldobler and Wilson *Journey to the Ants* page 55

[40] Holldobler and Wilson *Journey to the Ants* page 55

[41] Edward O Wilson *In Search of Nature* Penguin Books, London, England, 1996 page 64

[42] Wilson *In Search of Nature* page 66

[43] Wilson *In Search of Nature* page 67-68

[44] *Oxford Dictionary of Biology* Fourth Edition, Oxford University Press, Oxford, 2000

[45] Gordon Dickinson and Kevin Murphy *Ecosystems: A functional approach* Routledge, London and New York 1998 page 20

[46] Dickinson and Murphy *Ecosystems* page 30

[47] Jones, Allan M *Environmental Biology* Routledge, London and New York 1997 page 61

[48] Osborne, Patrick L *Tropical Ecosystems and Ecological Concepts* Cambridge University Press, Cambridge, United Kingdom 2000 pages 242-256

[49] Jones 1997, page 111

[50] Osborne 2000 page 98-99

[51] Osborne 2000 page 104

[52] Osborne 2000 page 250

[53] de Waal, Frans *The Ape and the Sushi Master: Cultural Reflections by a Primatologist* Penguin Books, London 2001 page 115

[54] de Waal, Frans *The Ape and the Sushi Master* page 119

[55] de Waal, Frans *The Ape and the Sushi Master* page 122

[56] Dusenbery, David B *Life at Small Scale: The Behaviour of Microbes* Scientific American Library, New York page 201

[57] Jones, Steve *Almost Like a Whale: The Origin of Species Updated* Transworld Publishers, London, 1999 page xxiv

[58] Charles Darwin *The Origin of Species by Means of Natural Selection or the Preservation of Favoured Races in the Struggle for Life* Mentor Edition with an Introduction by Sir Julian Huxley, New York, New York 1958 page 88-89

[59] Darwin *The Origin of Species* page 124

[60] Darwin *The Origin of Species* page 91-92

[61] Lewens, Tim *Organisms and Artifacts: Design in Nature and Elsewhere* MIT Press, Cambridge Massachusetts, London, England 2004 page 1

[62] Lewens, *Organisms and Artifacts* page 2

[63] Dawkins, Richard *The Blind Watchmaker* Penguin Books 1986 page 1

[64] Merchant, Carolyn *Reinventing Eden: The Fate of Nature in Western Culture* Routledge, New York and London 2003 page 76

[65] Dawkins, Richard *The Selfish Gene* Oxford University Press, Oxford, New York, 1976 page 2

[66] Gottlieb, Roger S *A Greener Faith: Religious Environmentalism and Our Planet's Future* Oxford University Press 2006

[67] Gottlieb *A Greener Faith* page 22

---

[68] Haught, John F "Darwin, Design and Divine Providence" in William A Dembski and Michael Ruse (ed) *Debating Design: From Darwin to DNA* Cambridge University Press 2004 page 244
[69] Polkinghorne, John "The Inbuilt Potentiality of Creation" in Dembski and Ruse *Debating Design* page 256
[70] Noble *The Music of Life* page 7
[71] Rose *Lifelines* pages 138-139
[72] Rensberger *Life Itself* page 93
[73] Rensberger *Life Itself* page 95
[74] Jones *Environmental Biology* page 20
[75] Maynard Smith and Szathmary *The Origins of Life* page 133
[76] Maynard Smith and Szathmary *The Origins of Life* page 133
[77] Maynard Smith and Szathmary *The Origins of Life* pages 3-4
[78] Maynard Smith and Szathmary *The Origins of Life* pages 7-8
[79] Turner, J Scott *The Tinkerer's Accomplice: How design emerges from life itself* Harvard University Press, Cambridge, Massachusetts 2007 page 1
[80] Corning *Nature's Magic* page 2
[81] Damasio, Antonio *The Feeling of What Happens: Body and Emotion in the Making of Consciousness* William Heinman, London, 2000 page 136
[82] Conway Morris *Life's Solutions* page 14
[83] Conway Morris *Life's Solutions* pages 11-12
[84] Conway Morris *Life's Solutions* page 12
[85] Conway Morris *Life's Solutions* page 12

Chapter Two: Value

[86] Grayling, Anthony C *What is Good? The Search for the Best Way to Live* Weidenfeld and Nicholson, Great Britain 2003 page 1
[87] Grayling *What is Good* page 7
[88] Grayling *What is Good* page 1
[89] Darwin *The Origin of Species* page 89 (my emphasis)
[90] Darwin *The Origin of Species* page 91 (my emphasis)
[91] Darwin *The Origin of Species* page 91 (my emphasis)
[92] Darwin *The Origin of Species* page 92
[93] Darwin *The Origin of Species* page 96
[94] Darwin *The Origin of Species* page 111
[95] Darwin *The Origin of Species* page 89
[96] Darwin *The Origin of Species* page 106
[97] Darwin *The Origin of Species* page 89
[98] Darwin *The Origin of Species* page 91
[99] Darwin *The Origin of Species* page 91

[100] Sterelny, Kim and Griffiths, Paul *Sex and Death: An Introduction to Philosophy and Biology* The University of Chicago Press, Chicago and London 1999 page 388
[101] Sterelny and Griffiths *Sex and Death* page 385
[102] Ayala, Francisco "Design without Designer: Darwin's Greatest Discovery" in Dembski and Ruse *Debating Design* page 58
[103] Dawkins, Richard *The Blind Watchmaker* Penguin Books London, England, 1988 page 9
[104] Lee "The Source and Locus of Intrinsic Value" page 156
[105] Holmes Rolston III "Value in Nature and the Nature of Value" page 17
[106] Mackie, John *Ethics: Inventing Right and Wrong* Penguin Books Middlesex, England 1977, page 15
[107] Mackie *Ethics* page 15
[108] Mackie *Ethics* page 16
[109] Mackie *Ethics* page 18
[110] Mackie *Ethics* page 35
[111] Mackie *Ethics* page 25
[112] Mackie *Ethics* page 26
[113] Mackie *Ethics* page 27
[114] Mackie *Ethics* page 17
[115] Mackie *Ethics* pages 36-37
[116] Mackie *Ethics* page 38
[117] Mackie *Ethics* page 40
[118] Mackie *Ethics* page 38
[119] Johnson, Lawrence E *A Morally Deep World: An Essay on Moral Significance and Environmental Ethics* Cambridge University Press Cambridge UK 1991 page 143
[120] Platts, Mark *Ways of Meaning: An Introduction to a Philosophy of Language* Routledge and Kegan Paul, London, England 1979
[121] Platts *Ways of Meaning* pages 255-59
[122] O'Neill, John "The Varieties of Intrinsic Value" in Andrew Light and Holmes Rolston III *Environmental Ethics: An Anthology* Blackwell Publishing 2003 page 131
[123] O'Neill "The Varieties of Intrinsic Value" page 131-132
[124] O'Neill "The Varieties of Intrinsic Value" page 132
[125] Dawkins, Richard *The Blind Watchmaker* Penguin Books, London, England 1986 page 9
[126] Dawkins *The Blind Watchmaker* page 9
[127] Darwin *The Origin of Species* page 91-92
[128] Darwin *The Origin of Species* page 126
[129] Lee, Keekok "The Source and Locus of Intrinsic Value: A Re-examination" pages 156-157
[130] Taylor, Paul W *Respect for Nature: A Theory of Environmental Ethics* Princeton University Press, Princeton New Jersey 1986 page 148
[131] Lee "The Source and Locus of Intrinsic Value: A Re-examination"

Chapter Three: Ethics

[132] Schweitzer, Albert *The Philosophy of Civilisation* Chapter 26 entitled "The Ethics of Reverence for Life" reproduced in Marvin Meyer and Kurt Bergel *Reverence for Life: The Ethics of Albert Schweitzer for the twenty-first century* Syrcuse University Press page 72

[133] Taylor, Paul *Respect for Nature: A Theory of Environmental Ethics* Princeton University Press, Princeton, New Jersey 1986 page 172

[134] Taylor *Respect for Nature* page 173

[135] Taylor *Respect for Nature* page 179

[136] Harman, Gilbert *The Nature of Morality: An Introduction to Ethics* Oxford University Press, New York 1977 pages 117-123

[137] Harman *The Nature of Morality* page 120

[138] Jones, Allen M *Environmental Biology* Routledge, London, England 1997 page 60

[139] Dickenson, George and Murphy, Kevin *Ecosystems: A functional approach* Routledge, London, England 1998 pages 172

[140] Jones *Environmental Biology* page 186

[141] Jones *Environmental Biology* pages 61-62

[142] Jones *Environmental Biology* page 61

[143] Jones *Environmental Biology* pages 112-113

[144] Schweitzer *The Philosophy of Civilisation* page 75

[145] Jones *Environmental Biology* page 22

[146] Schweitzer *The Philosophy of Civilisation* page 80

[147] Cited in Meyer, Marvin and Bergel, Kurt *Reverence for Life: The Ethics of Albert Schweitzer for the twenty-first century* pages 33-34

[148] Schweitzer *The Philosophy of Civilisation* page 73

[149] Schweitzer *The Philosophy of Civilisation* page 80

[150] Schweitzer *The Philosophy of Civilisation* page 80

[151] Cited in Meyer and Bergel *Reverence for Life* page 34

[152] Singer, Peter "The Place of Nonhumans in Environmental Issues" in Light, Andrew and Holmes Rolston III *Environmental Ethics: An Anthology* Blackwell Publishing Malden USA 2003 page 60

[153] Johnson Lawrence E *A Morally Deep World: An Essay on Moral Significance and Environmental Ethics* Cambridge University Press 1991

[154] Taylor *Respect for Nature* Page 239

[155] Taylor *Respect for Nature* page 219

[156] Schweitzer *The Philosophy of Civilisation* page 73

[157] Thich Nhat Hanh *The Blooming of a Lotus: Guided Meditation Exercises for Healing and Transformation* Beacon Press, Boston Massachusetts 1993 page 132

[158] Thich Nhat Hanh *The Blooming of a Lotus* page 132

[159] Thich Nhat Hanh *The Blooming of a Lotus* page 134

[160] Thich Nhat Hanh *The Heart of the Buddha's Teaching: Transforming Suffering into Peace, Joy and Liberation: The Four Noble Truths, The

Noble Eightfold Path and Other Basic Buddhist Teachings Parallax Press, Berkeley, California pages 43-44

[161] Taylor *Respect for Nature* Page 203-204

[162] Taylor *Respect for Nature* Page 200

[163] Widmaier, Eric *Why Geese Don't Get Obese (And We Do): How Evolution's Strategies for Survival Affect Our Everyday Lives* W H Freeman and Company New York 1999 page 18

[164] Widmaier *Why Geese Don't Get Obese* page 23

[165] Steve Jones *Almost Like a Whale: The Origin of Species Updated* Transworld Publishers, London page 24

[166] Flannery, Tim *The Future Eaters: An ecological history of the Australasian lands and people* Reed New Holland, Sydney, Australia 1994

[167] Flannery *The Future Eaters* pages 157-158,

[168] Diamond, Jared *The Rise and Fall of the Third Chimpanzee: How our animal heritage affects the way we live* Vintage London 2002 page 39

[169] Flannery *The Future Eaters* page 158

[170] Diamond *The Rise and Fall of the Third Chimpanzee* page 40

[171] Diamond *The Rise and Fall of the Third Chimpanzee* page 41

[172] Diamond *The Rise and Fall of the Third Chimpanzee* page 42

[173] Diamond *The Rise and Fall of the Third Chimpanzee* page 27

[174] Flannery *The Future Eaters* page 159

[175] Flannery *The Future Eaters* page 160

[176] Flannery *The Future Eaters* page 161

[177] Flannery *The Future Eaters* page 161

[178] Flannery *The Future Eaters* page 162

[179] Suzuki, David *Earth Time* Allen and Unwin, Sydney page 117

[180] Leakey, Richard and Lewin, Roger *The Sixth Extinction: Biodiversity and its Survival* Phoenix, London 1995 page 233

[181] Leakey and Lewin *The Sixth Extinction* page 241

[182] Leakey and Lewin *The Sixth Extinction* page 237

[183] Curry, Patrick *Ecological Ethics: An Introduction* Polity Press, Cambridge 2006 page 13

[184] Smil, Vaclav *Energy at the Crossroads: Global perspectives and uncertainties* Massachusetts Institute of Technology Press, Cambridge, Massachusetts 2003 page 207

[185] Smil *Energy at the Crossroads* pages 272-273

[186] Smil *Energy at the Crossroads* page 284

[187] Curry *Ecological Ethics* page 13

[188] Smil *Energy at the Crossroads* page 105

[189] Smil *Energy at the Crossroads* page 105

[190] Clark, Duncan *The Rough Guide to Ethical Living* November 2006, Rough Guides Ltd London page 189

[191] Clark *The Rough Guide to Ethical Living* page 189

[192] Clark *The Rough Guide to Ethical Living* page 178

[193] Clark *The Rough Guide to Ethical Living* page 182

[194] Noske, Barbara *Beyond Boundaries: Humans and Animals* Black Rose Books, Montreal, Canada 1997 page 22
[195] Noske *Beyond Boundaries* page 14
[196] Noske *Beyond Boundaries* page 14-15
[197] Noske *Beyond Boundaries* page 17
[198] Noske *Beyond Boundaries* page 18-19
[199] Clark *The Rough Guide to Ethical Living* page 184
[200] Clark *The Rough Guide to Ethical Living* page 188

Chapter Four: Human Flourishing

[201] Kraut, Richard *What is Good and Why: The Ethics of Well-Being* Harvard University Press, Cambridge Massachusetts, 2007 page 5
[202] Johnson, Lawrence E *A Morally Deep World: An Essay on Moral Significance and Environmental Ethics* Cambridge University Press, Cambridge, England 1997 page 143
[203] Hans-Georg Gademar *The Enigma of Health: The Art of Healing in a Scientific Age* Polity Press Cambridge UK page 36
[204] Turner, J Scott *The Tinkerer's Accomplice: How design emerges from life itself* Harvard University Press, Cambridge, Massachusetts 2007 page 146
[205] Kraut *What is Good and Why* page 5
[206] Hagen, Edward "What is Evolutionary Psychology?" http://www.anth.ucsb.edu/projects/human/epfaq/ep.html
[207] Rand, Ayn *The Virtue of Selfishness: A new concept of egoism* A Signet Book from New American Library 1964 page 17
[208] *Macquarie Dictionary*
[209] Johnson *A Morally Deep World* page 147
[210] Birch, Charles *On Purpose* University of New South Wales Press, Sydney, Australia 1990 page 8
[211] Maynard Smith and Szathmary *The Origins of Life* page 19
[212] Maynard Smith and Szathmary *The Origins of Life* page 20
[213] Thomas *Trees: Their Natural History* page 154
[214] Thomas *Trees: Their Natural History* page 140
[215] Corning *Holistic Darwinism* page 296
[216] Corning *Holistic Darwinism* page 296
[217] Plato *The Symposium* translated by Walter Hamilton Penguin Books, England, 1951 page 88
[218] Plato *The Republic* Translated with an introduction by Desmond Lee, Penguin Books, Second Edition (Revised) England 1974 page 215
[219] Plato *The Republic* page 216
[220] Ralston Saul, John *On Equilibrium* Penguin Books 2001 page 13
[221] Plato *The Republic* page 218

[222] Plato *The Republic* page 219

[223] Plato *The Republic* page 221

[224] Kraut *What is Good and Why* page 32

[225] Kraut *What is Good and Why* page 157

[226] Darwin, Charles *The Origin of Species by Means of Natural Selection or the Preservation of Favoured Races in the Struggle for Life* Mentor, New York 1958 page 131

[227] Darwin *The Origin of Species* page 131-132

[228] Davies, Paul *The Fifth Miracle: The Search for the Origin of Life* Allen Lane, The Penguin Press, Melbourne, Victoria page 42

[229] Davies *The Fifth Miracle* Paul Davies *The Fifth Miracle* page 42

[230] Margulis, Lynn *The Symbiotic Planet: A new look at evolution* Weidenfeld and Nicolson, London 1998 page 52

[231] Margulis, Lynn and Sagan, Dorion *What is Life?* University of California Press, Berkeley and Los Angeles, California 1995 page 55

[232] Margulis and Sagan *What is Life?* Page 44

[233] Margulis and Sagan *What is Life?* Page 44

[234] Thich Nhat Hanh *Plum Village Chanting and Recitation Book* Parallax Press, Berkeley, California 2000 "The Three Earth Touchings" page 33

[235] Margulis and Sagan *What is Life?* Page 55

[236] Thich Nhat Hanh *Plum Village Chanting and Recitation Book* "The Three Earth Touchings" page 34

[237] Thich Nhat Hanh *Plum Village Chanting and Recitation Book* "The Three Earth Touchings" page 33

[238] Thich Nhat Hanh *Plum Village Chanting and Recitation Book* "The Three Earth Touchings" page 33

[239] Margulis, Lynn and Sagan, Dorion *Microcosmos: Four Billion Years of Evolution from Our Microbial Ancestors* University of California Press, Berkeley and Los Angeles, California 1997 page 77

[240] Margulis and Sagan *Microcosmos* page 128

[241] Margulis and Sagan *Microcosmos* page 78

[242] Vernadsky, Vladimir *The Biosphere* in Salisbury, Frank (ed) *Geochemistry and the Biosphere: Essays by Vladimir I. Vernadsky* Synergistic Press, Santa Fe, New Mexico 2007 section 158 page 401

[243] Vernadsky *A few words about the Noosphere* in Salisbury, Frank (ed) *Geochemistry and the Biosphere: Essays by Vladimir I. Vernadsky* Synergistic Press, Santa Fe, New Mexico 2007 Section 10 page 414

[244] Vernadsky *A few words about the Noosphere* Section 3 page 407

[245] Vernadsky *The Biosphere* page 301

[246] Vernadsky *The Biosphere* page 302

[247] Vernadsky *The Biosphere* Section 22 pages 252-253

[248] Vernadsky *The Biosphere* Section 3 page 229

[249] Vernadsky *The Biosphere* Section 65, page 304

[250] Vernadsky *The Biosphere* Section 156 page 398

[251] Vernadsky *The Biosphere* Section 25 page 256

[252] Ferry, Luc *The New Ecological Order* translated into English by Carol Volk The University of Chicago Press, Chicago and London 1992 page xxi

[253] Ferry *The New Ecological Order* page xxi

[254] Seligman, Martin *Authentic Happiness: Using the new positive psychology to realize your potential for lasting fulfilment* Random House, Sydney, Australia 2002 pages 62-82

[255] Seligman *Authentic Happiness* pages 83-101

[256] Seligman *Authentic Happiness* pages 102-121

[257] Seligman *Authentic Happiness* page 11

[258] Seligman *Authentic Happiness* pages 141-145

[259] Seligman *Authentic Happiness* page 13

Chapter Five: Morality

[260] *The Macquarie Dictionary*

[261] Corning, Peter A *Holistic Darwinism: Synergy, Cybernetics and Bioeconomics of Evolution* The University of Chicago Press 2005 page 5

[262] Corning *Holistic Darwinism* page 4

[263] Williams, Bernard *Ethics and the Limits of Philosophy* Fontana Press/Collins 1985 page 174

[264] Williams *Ethics and the Limits of Philosophy* page 1

[265] Maynard Smith, John and Szathmary, Eors *The Origins of Life: From the birth of life to the origin of language* Oxford University Press, Oxford 1999 page 17

[266] Maynard Smith and Szathmary *The Origins of Life* page 21

[267] Maynard Smith and Szathmary *The Origins of Life* page 96

[268] Maynard Smith and Szathmary *The Origins of Life* page 23

[269] Maynard Smith and Szathmary *The Origins of Life* page 96

[270] Maynard Smith and Szathmary *The Origins of Life* page 99

[271] *Molecular Expressions Cell Biology: Mitochondria* http://micro.magnet.fsu.edu/cells/mitochondria/mitochondria.html

[272] Maynard Smith and Szathmary *The Origins of Life* pages 59-60

[273] Maynard Smith and Szathmary *The Origins of Life* page 59

[274] Margulis, Lynn and Sagan, Dorion *Microcosmos: Four Billion Years of Microbial Evolution* University of California Press, Berkeley, 1986 page 128

[275] University of Texas Medical Branch, Cell Biology Graduate Program "The Mitochondrial Life Cycle" http://cellbio.utmb.edu/cellbio/mitoch2.htm page 3

[276] University of Texas Medical Branch, Cell Biology Graduate Program "The Mitochondrial Life Cycle" pages 3-4

[277] *Molecular Expressions Cell Biology: Mitochondria* page 1

[278] Corning, Peter A *Nature's Magic: Synergy in evolution and the fate of mankind* Cambridge University Press, Cambridge, United Kingdom 2003 page 57
[279] Margulis and Sagan *Microcosmos* page 148
[280] Denis Noble *The Music of Life: Biology Beyond the Genome* Oxford University Press 2006 page 96
[281] Noble *The Music of Life* page 96
[282] Noble *The Music of Life* page 97
[283] Noble *The Music of Life* page 92
[284] Noble *The Music of Life* page 93
[285] Noble *The Music of Life* page 94
[286] Clark, William R *Sex and the Origins of Death* Oxford University Press, Oxford UK page 62
[287] Clark *Sex and the Origins of Death* page 62 footnote 1
[288] Clark *Sex and the Origins of Death* page 62
[289] Clark *Sex and the Origins of Death* pages 85
[290] Clark *Sex and the Origins of Death* page 86
[291] Clark *Sex and the Origins of Death* page 91
[292] Clark *Sex and the Origins of Death* page 100
[293] Clark *Sex and the Origins of Death* page 97
[294] Clark *Sex and the Origins of Death* page 93
[295] Clark *Sex and the Origins of Death* page 93
[296] Rose, Steven *Lifelines: Biology, Freedom, Determinism* Penguin Books 1997 page 139
[297] Corning *Holistic Darwinism* page 192
[298] Corning *Holistic Darwinism* page 195-196
[299] Corning *Holistic Darwinism* page 196
[300] Corning *Holistic Darwinism* pages 197-198
[301] Maynard Smith and Szathmary *The Origins of Life* page 133
[302] Maynard Smith and Szathmary *The Origins of Life* page 132
[303] Maynard Smith and Szathmary *The Origins of Life* page 133
[304] Bonnor, John Tyler *Life Cycles: Reflections of an Evolutionary Biologist* Princeton University Press, New Jersey, page 147-148
[305] Bonnor *Life Cycles* page 148
[306] Maynard Smith and Szathmary *The Origins of Life* page 127
[307] Corning *Nature's Magic* page 57
[308] Corning *Nature's Magic* page 120
[309] Noble *The Music of Life* page 96
[310] Noble *The Music of Life* page 50
[311] Corning *Holistic Darwinism* page 106
[312] Corning *Holistic Darwinism* page 36
[313] Noble *The Music of Life* page 53
[314] Wilson *In Search of Nature* page 67-68
[315] Noble *The Music of Life* page 96

[316] Grayling, Anthony *The Form of Things: Essays on Life, Ideas and Liberty in the 21ˢᵗ Century* Weidenfeld & Nicolson, Great Britain 2006 pages 9-10
[317] http://www.bls.gov/soc/

[318] Suzuki, David (with Amanda McConnell) *The Sacred Balance: Rediscovering our place in nature* Allen and Unwin, Australia 1997 page 9
[319] Corning *Holistic Darwinism* page 284
[320] Rawls, John *Political Liberalism* Columbia University Press, New York page 15
[321] Rawls *Political Liberalism* page 16
[322] From a discussion with Judith Flanagan
[323] Foot, Phillipa *Natural Goodness* Clarendon Press, Oxford UK 2001 page 45
[324] Corning *Holistic Darwinism* page 427
[325] Williams, Bernard *Ethics and the Limits of Philosophy* Fontana Press/Collins 1985 page 6
[326] Norman, Richard *The Moral Philosophers: An Introduction to Ethics* Second Edition Oxford University Press 1998 page 150-151
[327] Norman *The Moral Philosophers* page 151
[328] Norman *The Moral Philosophers* page 151
[329] Williams *Ethics and the Limits of Philosophy* page 177
[330] Margulis, Lynn and Sagan, Dorion *What is Life?* University of California Press, Berkeley California, 1995 pages 76-77
[331] Margulis and Sagan *What is Life?* Page 72-73
[332] Margulis and Sagan *What is Life?* Page 66
[333] Diamond, Jared *The Rise and the Fall of the Third Chimpanzee: How our animal heritage affects the way we live* First published 1991 Vintage edition 2002 page 165
[334] Diamond *The Rise and the Fall of the Third Chimpanzee* page 163
[335] Diamond *The Rise and the Fall of the Third Chimpanzee* page 169
[336] Diamond *The Rise and the Fall of the Third Chimpanzee* page 169-70
[337] Diamond *The Rise and the Fall of the Third Chimpanzee* page 170-71
[338] Diamond *The Rise and the Fall of the Third Chimpanzee* page 171
[339] Diamond, Jared *Guns, Germs and Steel: A short history of everybody for the last 13,000 years* Vintage Books, Great Britain 1998 page 267
[340] Diamond *Guns, Germs and Steel* page 268
[341] Diamond *Guns, Germs and Steel* page 269
[342] Grayling *The Form of Things* page 56
[343] Grayling *The Form of Things* page 73

Conclusion

[344] Dawkins, Richard *The Selfish Gene* Oxford University Press, Oxford 1976 page 17

[345] Clark, William R *Sex and the Origins of Death* Oxford University Press, New York 1996 page 170

[346] Davies, Paul *The Fifth Miracle: The search for the origin of life* Allen Lane, The Penguin Press, 1998, page 8

[347] Cited in Noske 1997 page 74

[348] *Beyond Good and Evil* Section 9

[349] Thich Nhat Hanh *Old Path White Clouds: Walking in the footsteps of the Buddha* Parallax Press, Berkeley, California 1991 page 63

[350] Cited in Farrelly, Elizabeth *Blubberland: The dangers of happiness* A New South book, Published by the University of New South Wales 2007 page 34

[351] Thich Nhat Hanh *The Heart of the Buddha's Teaching: Transforming suffering into peace, joy and liberation* Parallax Press, Berkeley, California, 1998 page 59

[352] Carson, Rachel *The Sense of Wonder* Harper Collins, New York. 1965 Reprinted in 1998 page 76

[353] Carson *The Sense of Wonder* page 54

[354] Carson *The Sense of Wonder* page 67

[355] Carson Rachel *The Sense of Wonder* page 67

[356] Cupitt, Don Interview with Rachel Kohn on Radio National *The Spirit of Things* 1/12/2002

[357] Cupitt Interview with Rachel Kohn on Radio National *The Spirit of Things* 1/12/2002

www.ingramcontent.com/pod-product-compliance
Lightning Source LLC
Chambersburg PA
CBHW071212240726
48654CB00009B/743